Additional Praise for *Billion Dollar Green*

"A must-read book about the green revolution that crosses political lines and helps investors invest more wisely in green energy. Green energy is coming one way or the other. Tobin Smith shows you where it will land so you can profit. Absolutely fascinating read."

Louis Navellier
CIO of Navellier & Associates
Author of *The Little Book That Makes You Rich*

"There are a lot of stock market prognosticators out there but few are the real deal and Toby happens to be at the top of the list. Investors like Toby because of his wit and charm but everyone respects him because of his ability to see out further into the future than others. More importantly is with the rapid greening of capitlaism it's so important that investors truly understand how to capitalize. Toby explains the Eco Revolution and names the exact companies to be in order to profit from it."

Charles Payne
Founder & CEO
Wall Street Strategies

"Ride the green wave to success with this indispensible guide to the coming global economic transformation! As usual, Tobin Smith is ahead of the curve, synthesizing a complex theme into easy-to-understand, useful information for all investors."

Jill Schlesinger, CFP
Chief Investment Officer
StrategicPoint Investment Advisors

Billion Dollar Green

Billion Dollar Green

PROFIT FROM THE ECO REVOLUTION

Tobin Smith

with Jim Woods

WILEY

John Wiley & Sons, Inc.

For general information on our other products and services or for technical support, please contact our Customer Care Department within the United States at (800) 762-2974, outside the United States at (317) 572-3993 or fax (317) 572-4002.

Wiley also publishes its books in a variety of electronic formats. Some content that appears in print may not be available in electronic books. For more information about Wiley products, visit our web site at www.wiley.com.

Library of Congress Cataloging-in-Publication Data:

Smith, Tobin, 1957-
  Billion dollar green : profit from the eco revolution / Tobin Smith.
      p. cm.
  Includes index.
  ISBN 978-0-470-34377-7 (cloth)
    1. Clean energy industries.   2. Clean energy investment.   3. Investments.
  I. Title.
  HD9502.5.C54S65   2009
  333.79'4—dc22

                                                           2008036134

Printed in the United States of America

10 9 8 7 6 5 4 3 2 1

Contents

Foreword

I've been conserving energy and water since I was four.

Oh yes, as a child growing up in L.A. in the 1970s, many of us learned how to conserve before we learned how to read. I'll never forget my father marching us upstairs one day to show us how to put a brick in the toilet tank. My four siblings and I were enraptured. "It'll save water, kids. Because," he said very slowly so that we fully understood, "one day the world might not have enough clean water."

Listen, it wasn't exactly a news flash, even for this preschooler. We were already grappling with the drought back then . . . fending off dagger eyes from the San Francisco folks because Los Angeles was "stealing northern Californians' water." We battled yellowish-gray smog that prompted the infamous "smog alerts" screamed at us by *Eyewitness News* anchors every morning.

So I suppose you could say that from an early age I had a sense of what it meant to be "Green." But aside from my forward-thinking father and some of his friends—one of whom climbed up on his roof in Beverly Hills and installed solar panels 36 years ago and hasn't paid an electric bill since—most people following the Green movement were thought of by others as "those kooks in Topanga Canyon," or macramé-toting nature moms. I mean, could you really make a dime off Ed Begley Jr.'s idea to run his toaster by pedaling a stationary bicycle? C'mon. Making real green off being Green was never part of the equation. Until now.

Little did we know that we were on the very cusp of an idea that would take three more decades to really take hold. Now, as we face skyrocketing global energy, water, and food demand, suddenly the world has woken up. But as the proverbial sun rises on this idea whose time seems to have finally come, it has brought along the realization that there's a massive land grab going on in Green Land.

Enter Tobin Smith. What Tobin has done for you with *Billion Dollar Green* is not only generous, but genius as well. He's done the heavy-lifting homework for the legions of investors who rightly believe there's money to be made off the Movement but just don't know where to begin. If you're one of those folks who's just now realizing that Green technology—wind, solar, biofuel, Green nano-technology—are investments you should have in your portfolio, a mere scratching of the surface has probably revealed that while world governments were fiddling, Rome wasn't the only city burning. New York, Beijing, Moscow, Los Angeles, Tokyo, and the rest have become polluted and panicked.

The good news is that smart people everywhere weren't waiting for world leaders to lead. They have been starting up companies around the world that could very well solve most, if not all of our problems. Legions of brilliant scientists and entrepreneurs have been at it for years, and many of them have begun companies that are ripe for your investment portfolio. But caution is the keyword. We all know how many dot-coms sprouted up in the late 1990s. And, conversely, we know how many of them failed. Tobin has pinpointed the Green names he feels have a fighting chance and are worth a look for your portfolio.

Is global warming a reality? I'll leave you with this: last year I had a chance to ask the world's second-richest man whether he believes global warming is real. Warren Buffett also happens to be arguably the greatest investor of our time. He didn't pause for long before telling me, "Well, Liz, we don't really know. But since we only have one planet, we'd better err on the side of the planet."

LIZ CLAYMAN
September 2008
New York, New York

An Opportunity Too Big to Miss

If you've just picked up this book, most likely you're of a mind that investing in alternative, clean, green, and energy technologies as well as their many related sectors is an opportunity too big to miss out on.

To that I say: Wise decision!

You see, it's not hyperbole to believe that the greatest wealth creation wave since the discovery of oil is upon us right here, right now—and more importantly, will likely be with us for the next two decades and beyond.

Moreover, your decision to read this book is also a great one—if I may be so bold as to say so myself—because it will give you a quick, painless, and very enjoyable education in the opportunities that a new greener world has brought forth.

Simply put; if you want to learn about the green investment arena, you've come to the right place.

But hey, why should you take my advice on how to approach this enormous investment opportunity? Well, because I've seen this transformation technology movie before, and I know how to make the story turn out the way you want.

You see, analyzing transformation change is what we do at ChangeWave Research, the global investment research company I founded 10 years ago. We have always been early to identify the major technological and regulatory shifts of the late twentieth and early twenty-first centuries. Because of our ability to identify these transformational shifts, we have grown into one of the largest independent investment research firms in the world.

From the rise of the Internet to the rise of satellite radio, and most recently the rise of alternative energy technology, we have consistently chosen the winning horses in the transformational technology stakes.

Our edge in accomplishing this feat is our 15,000-member investment research and analysis network, the ChangeWave Alliance. With this volunteer army of scientists, geophysicists, engineers, entrepreneurs, physicians, and sales and marketing professionals of all stripes, we are able to get a ground-level view of emerging transformational waves way before most other analysts.

It was from this most august group that we were early to identify the transformation in the supply/demand curve for oil and natural gas. The secular transformation of China and India from exporters of oil and coal to fast-growing importers is one major leg of the alternative energy investment thesis—and it's a leg we identified way before the news was fit to print.

Intelligence reports gleaned early on concerning energy supply and demand from our network of geologists and energy professionals got us early into mostly unheard of energy exploration and production companies based around the world. We were early into the tar sands of Canada, and early into technology companies that have revolutionized the craft and science of energy exploration.

It was this early recognition of the secular shift in the supply and demand for fossil fuels in the new, twenty-first century global economy that led us to conclude that, for the very first time, economics—not just environmentalism or tree-hugging wannabes—would drive the decades-plus secular transition to alternative energy technology.

In my ChangeWave Investing advisory service, we have already earned significant triple-digit profits investing in the "arms dealer" plays on first-generation green energy companies. But the profits in the second- and third-generation green energy space will be measured in thousand percent gains. Why? Well, because we have tens of trillions of dollars in growth still to come.

It's those second- and third-generation companies—the technologies that compete favorably with the costs of energy from fossil fuels without government subsidies—where the greatest investment profits will be made.

I've looked at hundreds of private and public green energy companies, and have visited dozens of these second- and third-generation companies. Just like the boom in the Internet and unconventional energy spaces, I have made significant personal investments in both public and privately held companies developing amazing technology designed to help solve the world's energy challenges.

I have personally earned seven-figure wealth investing in transformational change, and perhaps that's the most important reason of all to at least give my analysis of this—the mother of all technology transformations—a thorough read.

Making small—and not so small—fortunes investing in transformational technologies is really what my life's work is all about. The best advice I can give you on making your fortune in this amazing opportunity is to read this book and learn the basics, including the lingo and general concepts in all of the various green sectors.

Then you can start to build your list of existing companies, and new, yet-to-go-public companies in the various green sectors we cover, including; solar, wind, biofuels, power grid infrastructure, solid-state lighting, energy storage, electric vehicles, and, of course, the core arms dealers supplying goods needed to make the world's green dreams a reality.

Finally, you'll want to make your investments early in the life cycle of the new and existing players coming to prominence in this dynamic marketplace. You'll want to find companies with the lowest-cost solutions, the greatest market dominance, the highest efficiency, and the strongest patents in their respective fields.

But, hey, I realize I am getting a bit ahead of myself here. Those of you who are familiar with me and my sometimes unbridled enthusiasm for all things investing will understand that it's all part of what makes me who I am. Another thing that makes me who I am is my intense commitment to you, the individual investor.

The way I see it, this book is literally the first step on your path to a lifetime of wealth. And as any seasoned traveler knows, the first step is always the most exciting. So, please put one foot in front of the other, and let's take that first step down the green brick road.

—TOBIN SMITH

Billion Dollar Green

It's a Green, Green, Green World

Everywhere I look, I see green.

No, I am not admitting to some overwhelming sense of jealousy inherent in the fabric of my being. I am talking about the ubiquity of all things "green" in our society intended to protect and improve our environment.

I suspect that like me you have already noticed in recent years the tremendous attention given to all things green. Books, magazine articles, newspapers, TV, radio, investment advisors, and even the political class—maybe especially them—have all put green issues into the forefront of the world's collective conscience. In fact, the tremendous focus on green has now become so pervasive that nearly everyone reading this can think of many examples of how the Green Revolution is already influencing how they live. Indeed, "going green" is now considered a virtuous pursuit that we all must embark on. The new awareness that we must go green is not just a matter of making the world a cleaner, more livable, and better place. It is about ensuring the very survival of our species.

I know that sounds dramatic and, quite frankly, it is very dramatic. However, it's dramatic for a good reason.

Think about it. What is more important than ensuring the world has enough energy to thrive? What is more important than preventing the world from suffocating under a blanket of carbon emissions?

This means something very specific to the investor. Quite simply, going green could be the greatest wealth-building opportunity of the twenty-first century. Indeed, the greening of just about everything nowadays means that the entire game is changing when it comes to investing in clean tech, alternative energy, or green-related companies. I use these three terms to describe this green path to gold because investing in this sprawling, multiheaded, multifaceted, and often nuanced space has become much larger than just clean energy technologies. In this book I use the term *green investing* to cover the entire gamut of profitable opportunities directly and tangentially related to alternative energy and its many offshoots.

What Drives the Green Wave?

I am not exaggerating in the least when I say that the global move toward all things green has the potential to be just as big, if not bigger, than the tremendous wealth-producing effect of the microchip.

But what is driving this green opportunity besides the new "awareness," the realization that green is good?

The simple answer is economics.

Now when I say economics, it is not just the cost of specific energy components such as oil. I mean the complex interactions between the rising costs for existing energy assets derived from fossil fuels and the decreasing costs of alternative green sources.

This complex economic interaction has a lot to do with the increased world demand for energy and the need to find a supply of energy. Of course, the issue of climate change and the costs to society associated with global warming is also a big part of the economics driving the green energy wave.

Then you have the economics of consumer demand. The world is realizing that green is good, and that means consumers are choosing goods and services increasingly because of their green characteristics.

Finally, you have a tremendous amount of investment capital pouring into all things green in search of a big return. As that capital flows, new technologies that were once relegated to the drawing board now have the financial means to make it to the marketplace.

I think the increasing amounts of venture capital going into green companies and technologies means that the smart money is betting on a greener future. That means you, the individual investor, will have ample opportunity to pick and choose from the best of the best when it comes to companies in many burgeoning green industries.

Now let's take a quick glance at some of the economic drivers to see why this "green wave" has become so incredibly powerful.

An Oily Proposition

I can remember in 2006 when I was touting $60-a-barrel oil as the cure for $60 oil. Today, that $60-a-barrel mark is a fond and very distant memory. Oil has blown past the $100-a-barrel mark in the first quarter, 2008; a level many Wall Street professionals and petroleum industry analysts didn't think would come to pass for another decade.

I am of the opinion now that $60 oil is an artifact, and that we will never see that level of cost for petroleum again.

Why will oil likely remain so expensive?

The answer here is not just a matter of increasing demand from the growing economies of the world—although that, too, is a major driving force behind increasing oil costs. But the one real key to the economics of oil is the increasing cost of finding and producing new light, sweet crude (low-sulfur oil needed by 90 percent of the world's refineries) outside of Saudi Arabia and Russia.

Discovery and production costs for new crude oil (mostly from deep water wells) are helping push prices to over $100 a barrel. We are also depleting existing sweet crude reservoirs faster than we are replacing them—about 1.5 times faster, according to the latest industry estimates.

So understand this: If 90 percent of the world's oil refiners need low-sulfur oil, and most of the spare capacity and new oil coming from the Organization of Petroleum Exporting Countries (OPEC) is sour crude, we have a supply-and-demand problem in sweet crude.

The key point here to understand is that virtually all of the easy-to-find, easy-to-extract crude oil has already been found. Sure, there are still plenty of proven reserves of oil around the world, but they are located in either very remote locations or in environments that are very hostile to operate in. This means the cost of extracting this oil is going to rise—and hence the current high cost of oil. But supply-and-demand issues are not the only factors driving oil prices higher. The politics of oil dominate the discussion, and with oil prices controlled largely by the OPEC cartel, oil prices can keep going up regardless of organic supply/demand dynamics.

Then there is the security issue with respect to oil. Given the fact that much of the world's oil is located in countries that are less than friendly or even downright hostile toward the United States—Iran comes to mind here—any political move to disrupt the flow of oil could really cause the price per barrel to surge.

The bottom line here, given the aforementioned factors, is that oil prices are not likely to go significantly lower anytime soon. Sure, there may be a pullback in crude oil prices from the record highs we hit in early 2008, but with demand for oil soaring, and with the easy-to-extract, "cheap" oil nearly gone, the world will have to cope with higher oil prices for decades to come.

Those higher oil prices mean that alternative energy sources will continue growing in popularity, and it means that their costs will continue coming closer and closer to parity with traditional sources.

We Want Our NRG!

Remember that tagline from the Music Television network back in the 1980s—"I want my MTV"?

Today, the world can be heard making a similar proclamation, but this time it is—"We want our NRG!" Here *NRG* is just my way of saying *energy*.

I've alluded to it already, but today the global demand for all energy is growing at a blistering pace. According to forecasts from the International Energy Agency (IEA), world energy demand for energy will increase by 55 percent from 2005 to 2030, or at an annual rate of 1.8 percent.

Much of this demand growth is coming from China, India, and other developing nations. As these hugely populated countries make the transition from largely rural to largely industrial nations, worldwide demand for energy is going to continue growing.

Providing the world's hefty appetite for energy will be a challenge, not only because the growing beast that is these developing nations will need more and more resources, but also because these traditional resources come with a price tag.

That price tag is more and more greenhouse gases, and that is something virtually nobody wants.

A Cleaner Future

When you burn organic matter—be it wood, oil, coal, or natural gas—you get carbon as a by-product. That carbon goes into the earth's atmosphere and creates a situation which either causes—or at least contributes—to increases in the planet's surface temperature.

That temperature increase across the globe could have a deleterious effect on the world as we know it. Now, I suspect you have heard the doomsday scenarios reflected by the Al Gore camp as to just how bad global warming could potentially be.

These chaos-ridden scenes where drought, famine, floods, and a host of other calamities afflict the planet are indeed very discomforting even for the harshest of skeptics.

But I am not going to argue the truth of the former vice president's claims, nor am I going to challenge or confirm the science behind his thesis. What I am telling you is that people are rightly concerned about this issue more than they have ever been before, and that concern is something you, the individual investor, can take advantage of.

The fact is that the world wants a cleaner future. We want to reduce our "carbon footprint," to quote a very fashionable term, and we want to make sure that the countries in the developing world don't throw caution to the wind with an unabashed and even reckless use of fossil fuels.

The only way to satiate the world's growing energy appetite while not creating a situation where we choke on our own carbon by-products is to make sure we employ as much green energy—and as many green products—as possible.

Green Is Getting Cost Competitive

As long as the price of oil and other fossil fuel energy sources such as natural gas and coal remains high—which it most likely will, given the demand drivers already mentioned—the price of alternative energy sources will get more and more competitive.

Indeed, the cost of green energy is likely to continue declining with new technologies coming on line, and as a general rule, we can safely say that as the price of fossil fuels goes up, the cost of alternative sources is—and will continue—coming down.

And as demand for green energy increases, production from green sources such as solar, wind, biofuels, and others will begin declining. Why is this so? Well, technology here is the key.

You see, there is no cost associated with the "fuel" of these green energy sources. The sun, wind, and heat generated from the earth's crust are all free commodities. Once you've figured out a way to harness these sources and deliver them to the market technologically, the cost will start to come down.

Also, there is a tendency in technologically driven industries to see the price of their products decline rapidly over time. We saw this in the computer industry, as the costs of both the microchip and computing power have experienced a steady decline over the past several decades.

This kind of price decline due to new technologies will no doubt occur in the green energy production segments, and that means clean energy will get more cost competitive with other legacy sources.

Mo' Money, Mo' Growth

In addition to technological improvements, another factor greasing the wheels of the green energy sector is *investment capital.*

According to the research group New Energy Finance, U.S.-based venture capital investments in energy technologies more than quadrupled from $599 million in 2000 to $2.7 billion in 2007. As a percentage of total venture capital, energy technology increased from well under 1 percent in 2000 to over 9 percent in 2007.

Between 2006 and 2007, venture capital investments in the U.S. clean energy space increased by more than 70 percent!

Remember that old adage "follow the money"? Well, that's exactly what we are doing here, and there is no doubt that the money is going toward all things green.

Want even more evidence to support the claim that dollars are flooding into the green energy? How about $150 billion?

That's the estimate on Wall Street regarding the new global investment in all green energy sectors in 2007.

All I can say to this is—wow!

Yet, in my opinion, we'll look back on this number and realize it was just a drop in a big green bucket.

According to the International Energy Agency, $16 trillion needs to be invested by 2030 to meet the growth in projected demand for electricity and fuel worldwide. That's about $600 billion a year.

I suspect much of that will go into green energy production, and that means growth in the space is going to be with us for a very long time.

The Greening of the Consumer

In the United States, people follow the hippest trends, and I can't think of any trend more pervasive nowadays than going green.

All kinds of products and all kinds of services have sprouted up offering green products to a green-conscious consumer. This desire to make the green choice—in many cases even when that choice means the consumer may have to pay a little more—is driving many buying decisions.

Everything from automobiles to food to clothing to appliances, the greener it is, the better we like it.

This greening of the consumer means there will be plenty of opportunities for growth in those sectors that cater to green-sensitive tastes.

Building a Green Portfolio

Imagine it's 1908, and a skinny, middle-aged man named Henry Ford asks if you want to invest in his new company that is going to mass produce something called a "horseless carriage."

Imagine too that you're given the opportunity to invest in a young oil company, the Texas Fuel Company (soon to be known as Texaco) and in Harvey Firestone's company, which makes the tires for the horseless carriages.

Then along comes a guy named Thomas Edison asking if you'd be interested in backing his new invention, the incandescent light bulb.

Those would have been fantastic investment opportunities, and they are similar to the opportunities we have today in the green investing revolution. The chance for you to build wealth for yourself, your children, and your children's children is here—and the beauty of it is we are just getting started.

When I tell you that the "green wave" is going to be far bigger than any other trend I've ever tracked, believe me, I'm not just blowing smoke. Today, remarkable change is sweeping the globe, and you can be sure that its momentum will only grow more powerful in 2008 and beyond.

From solar cell manufacturers to software companies that boost IT energy efficiencies, these firms have one thing in common: They are working overtime to quench the booming appetite of enterprises and their customers who are seeking to use energy, water, and other raw materials more efficiently and productively.

Environment Protection Becomes Big Bucks

Before 1850, the Earth's atmosphere contained about 280 parts per million of carbon dioxide. Then we began burning oil, gas, and coal. Now that figure is 380 parts per million. By 2050, it could reach 550 parts per million, according to the Intergovernmental Panel on Climate Change, the United Nations' scientific group that shared the 2007 Nobel Peace Prize with Al Gore.

The very large and growing environmental movement is no longer the domain of hippies and a clique of low-profile scientists. Concerns about climate change and its causes are now reported daily by mainstream media.

Green thinking is fast becoming institutionalized worldwide as multinational corporations adopt new, efficient production methods and governments mandate cleaner air and water.

More importantly for individuals and investors, there are "real" green companies making "real" profits in this new environment. And that means there are real opportunities to make big profits investing in "green companies," some of which will really surprise you.

The Goal of This Book

The goal of this book is twofold. First, I want to help you understand why the green wave has grown so strong in recent years, and why it will likely continue growing relentlessly for the next decade and well beyond.

Chapters 1 and 2 outline the catalysts driving the green wave forward, including world energy demand, carbon dioxide (CO_2) emission concerns and governmental mandates. We'll also take a look at the growth potential for the entire green market.

Beginning with Chapter 3 and continuing through Chapter 13, we get into the second goal of this book, which is to explore the possibilities, problems, profit potential, and key players in specific green sectors. These sectors include; transportation, solar, water, power grid management, eco-efficient IT, bioengineered solutions, biomass and biofuels, fuel cells and hybrid batteries, wind, green structures, food and green lifestyle products, and even old energy industries using new products and technologies to be green—and more importantly, to make green.

Chapter 14 shows you how to build your own green portfolio, and serves as a kind of green call to arms.

It's a brave new green world out there, and with a little knowledge and a bold sense of vision, you too can be green—and make the green.

CHAPTER 1

Catalyzing into Green

WHY, AND WHY NOW?

Everything's fine today, that is our illusion.

—Voltaire

So, why green, and why green now?

I've heard some people say that the greening of just about everything these days is simply a business ploy to sell more products. I've also heard the more cynical crowd tell me that green energy and green products are just feel-good marketing and public relations tools designed to make certain companies appear as though they're good citizens and caring custodians of the world.

Now I am not so Pollyannaish that I don't see that there is often more than a hint of truth to these claims. But despite the many companies and public officials engaging in green propaganda, there are real companies helping to solve real-world problems.

And what is catalyzing the world into a greener place. It is the massive challenges of what I call the "Big Three":

1. Rising global energy demand (particularly from China and India)
2. Energy security: the New Cold War
3. Carbon concerns

To be sure, covering the intimate details of each of these factors could take up an entire book on its own. So I'll restrict the discussion to the primary issues as to why the world is seeing the virtue of all things green.

Rising Global Energy Demand

So, we've heard a lot about this new era of the "global economy," an for the most part this is a fantastic circumstance that is helping many of the 6.6 billion residents of the planet to enjoy better living conditions. Of course, with the yin there's always a yang, and the yang here is a voracious and growing appetite for energy.

According to the Energy Information Administration (EIA)—a division of the U.S. Department of Energy (DOE)—in its *International Energy Outlook 2007* report, worldwide energy demand from 2004 to 2030 is projected to increase from 447 quadrillion Btu (British thermal units) in 2004 to 559 quadrillion Btu in 2015. That number then climbs to 702 quadrillion Btu in 2030—a 57 percent increase over the projected period (DOE/EIA-0484, 2007).

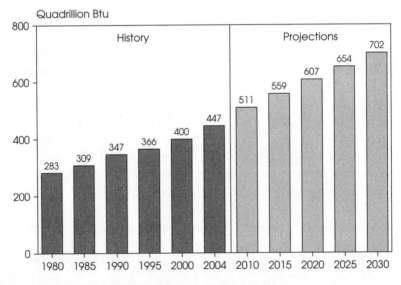

Figure 1.1   World Marketed Energy Consumption

Source: Figure 8 from EIA, *International Energy Outlook 2007* (Washington, D.C.: U.S. Department of Energy, May 2007), p. 5.

Figure 1.1 shows both historical demand trends worldwide, as well as the projections made by the EIA all the way out to 2030.

The largest projected increase in energy demand is for the non-OECD (Organisation for Economic Co-operation and Development) region. Countries outside the OECD, that is, developing countries such as China and India (more on them in a moment), have projected economic growth rates and more rapid population growth than the OECD nations. The appetite for energy in the non-OECD region is projected to grow at an average annual rate of 2.6 percent from 2004 through 2030. Growth in the developed and mature economies of the OECD region—Europe, the United States and others—is expected to be slower by comparison (DOE/EIA-0484, 2007).

Here the EIA projects energy use will grow at the much slower average rate of 0.8 percent until 2030. Interestingly, the energy appetite for the non-OECD region is projected to surpass that of the OECD region by 2010. By 2030 it could be as high as 35 percent greater (see Figure 1.2).

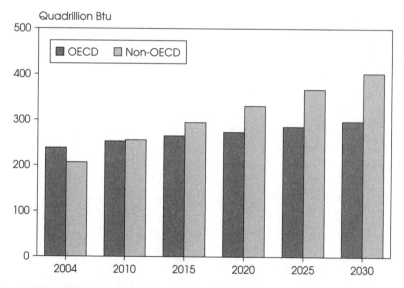

Figure 1.2   World Energy Use 2004–2030

Source: Figure 9 from EIA, *International Energy Outlook 2007* (Washington, D.C.: U.S. Department of Energy, May 2007), p. 6. What the EIA data projections mean is that the world will be consuming energy at a blistering pace for at least the next two decades, and likely well beyond that if the past is any kind of prelude to the future.

The Chindia Syndrome

The combined economic transformation going on in both China and India—or *Chindia* as I will refer to them in this book—is going to have a massive impact on the world's demand for energy.

In the case of Chindia, size definitely matters.

Growth in Chindia is occurring at breakneck speed and so has its appetite for fuel. As these countries become more capitalistic, richer, and increasingly industrialized, they are going to require the lifeblood of a flourishing society—and that lifeblood is more and more energy.

In fact, it's a general rule that the more industrialized a country is, and the richer it is, the greater the energy use on a per-capita-basis. That's why the very richest countries in the Western world have the highest per capita energy use.

And while we here in the West, and particularly in the United States, are accustomed to just flipping the light switch, jumping into our cars for a ride, and booting up our laptop computers, cell phones, and other modern conveniences, the citizens of Chindia are really just beginning to feel what's this is like on a society-wide basis.

The fact is that as Chindia grows, it will require more energy to power its offices, factories, homes, and cars. Now, on balance, I think this growth in Chindia is fantastic, especially for people who've largely spent nearly the entire twentieth century without the conveniences of the modern world.

According to the International Energy Agency (IEA), worldwide energy demand will be at least 50 percent higher than current levels by 2030 (note these levels are similar to the EIA, albeit slightly lower). I say at least, because that is the agency's most conservative projection. The interesting thing here is that because of its tremendous population and industrialization, Chindia is likely to account for 45 percent of this projected increase in demand.

It's hard to imagine anyone arguing that Chindia's growth won't lead to more energy consumption, but at what rate is this likely to occur? The answer depends on numerous factors. The biggest factor really depends on how quickly the region's economy expands.

The IEA projects China's primary energy demand will more than double from 2005 to 2030. That's translates into an average annual rate of growth of 3.2 percent. Keep in mind that China has approximately four times as many people as the United

States, and that demographic element—along with the nation's industrialization—will make it the world's largest energy consumer by about 2010. Compare that to just a few years ago in 2005, when U.S. demand was more than one third larger.

China's growth will be particularly intense in the period up to 2015. The IEA says by then, China's energy demand will grow by 5.1 percent per year. Once again, this will be largely driven by that country's industrial boom.

The other element to the Chindia contraction is, of course, India. Here too, we see huge economic expansion that will continue increasing energy demand. That increased demand will also continue boosting the country's share of global energy consumption.

Like China, the IEA projects energy demand in India will more than double by 2030, growing on average by 3.6 percent per year. So, as Chindia becomes a global megawatt vacuum, more and more energy will be needed. This increased demand will be with us for a while, and the only problem with it is that the energy will come primarily from one source, namely fossil fuels.

Where Does That Energy Come From?

An energy-hungry world needs to be fed, and for the next several decades, the primary feedstock for the world's energy is fossil fuels.

I know some of the more green-oriented readers will be upset by this. The reality is that the world will rely heavily on traditional carbon energy sources for as far out as we can see. This carbon cloud does, however, have a green lining, a lining we'll look at in great detail as this story unfolds.

Right now I want to show you where the world gets its energy and just how carbon dominant the energy landscape really is. In Figure 1.3, we can see precisely where the world has historically gotten its energy, and where we are likely to get that energy from out until 2030. As you can see, it's a carbon-oriented world, with fossil fuels continuing to supply most of the world's energy needs.

According to the EIA (2007), liquids here (which include oil and other petroleum products) will continue providing the largest share of world energy consumption over the projection period. But their share falls from 38 percent in 2004 to 34 percent in 2030. Why the decline? Well, one reason is that rising world oil prices are likely to curtail demand for liquids after 2015.

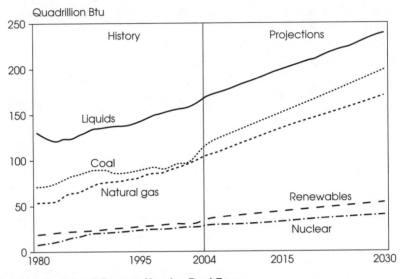

Figure 1.3   World Energy Use by Fuel Type

Source: Figure 11 from EIA, *International Energy Outlook 2007* (Washington, D.C.: U.S. Department of Energy, May 2007), p. 7.

Why will oil prices rise? See the box titled "The New Age of Oil."

Natural gas consumption is projected to grow about 1.9 percent per year on average until 2030, from about 100 trillion cubic feet in 2004 to 163 trillion cubic feet in 2030. In fact, natural gas will likely be the world's fastest-growing energy source for electricity generation.

Natural gas prices are much more of a regional issue than oil prices due to the availability worldwide, but at least in the United States, the price of domestic supplies is likely to continue trending higher.

Coal is yet another fossil fuel likely to increase in usage among the world's energy consumers. The EIA predicts coal use worldwide will increases by 37 quadrillion Btu from 2004 to 2015, and by another 48 quadrillion Btu from 2015 to 2030. The United States, China, and India will experience the vast majority of this increase in coal usage, accounting for about 90 percent of the total increase from 2004 to 2030.

Worldwide, electricity generation in 2030 is projected to total 30,364 billion kilowatt hours, nearly double the 2004 total of 16,424 billion kilowatt hours, according to the EIA. That is a whole lot

The New Age of Oil

The 2005 film *Syriana* is an extremely interesting treatment of the not-so-pretty geopolitical and corporate intrigue surrounding the battle for the greatest natural resource the world has ever known—oil.

In what would turn out to be an ironic coincidence, I happened to tune in to this film on cable TV. This was in March 2008, when oil prices hit new all-time highs of more than $100 a barrel. This confluence of events prompted me to ask myself if, years from now, I will look back at $100 oil as the good old inexpensive days.

Frighteningly, I think the answer is yes.

Why do I think we are in for more pain in the oil patch? Well, the simple answer is supply and demand. Diminishing supplies of low-cost oil coupled with a voracious world appetite for energy is an Economics 101 recipe for higher oil prices. Of course, the issues surrounding oil aren't simply a matter of supply and demand.

There are many other factors influencing oil prices, including geopolitical turmoil, geology, science, the emergence of China and India as economic power players, and the development of alternative energy sources.

To get a basic understanding of what is perhaps the most fundamental issue shaping this new age of oil, we must first understand the concept of peak oil. I suspect this may be a new idea for many of you, as the issue doesn't get the kind of attention in the mainstream media I think it deserves.

The term *peak oil* is widely used amongst petroleum industry observers as a way to basically describe the global maximum in conventional crude oil production. This peak in conventional crude oil production is predicted to happen in the not-too-distant future, and some analysts actually think we are now past the point of peak oil.

The peak oil theory states that once the global maximum in conventional crude oil production has been reached, global oil production will generally decline forever afterwards. That's forever, as in for the rest of time. What is scary about this theory is that its veracity will only become apparent some time after the point of peak oil has actually occurred.

According to some analysts, peak oil will occur when approximately half of the world's total oil reserves have been used up. The model used to think about the big picture is essentially an extrapolation from what happens to every individual oil field over time. You see, when you first start drilling in an oil field the costs of extracting that oil is relatively modest.

(Continues)

(Continued)

As the supply of oil in a given field dwindles, it becomes increasingly difficult to get the oil out of the ground. The more difficult the extraction process, the more costly it becomes. As the cost of extraction escalates, the less cost-effective it becomes to remove that oil from the ground. This increasing cost spiral continues until it becomes economically unfeasible to extract any more oil from a given field.

Apply this individual model to the entire world's oil supply and you begin to get a handle on the global peak oil theory. As you might expect, oil companies have to a great extent already extracted the easy-to-reach, cheap oil first. This was the oil found on land; near the earth's surface; under pressure so as to make it easy to tap; and the light and sweet crude (i.e., low sulfur content), which can easily be refined into gasoline. The remaining oil, sometimes offshore, far from markets, in smaller fields, and/or of lesser quality, was left for "later."

Well my friends, "later" is now.

According to *The Oil Drum* (www.theoildrum.com), on a worldwide basis the phenomenon of peak oil can be thought of as a crisis in resources needed to produce oil. As we deplete the large, easy-to-produce fields and move to ever-more-difficult fields, oil extraction takes more and more equipment like drilling rigs, more brain power in the form of petroleum engineers, and more investment capital to keep the whole ball game going. Eventually, we will reach a point where we deplete our equipment, trained and experienced personnel, as well as the dollars that make extraction viable.

When production begins to drop as a result of this combination of factors, we will have reached peak oil.

of energy needed in the coming years, and the fact is that only a fraction of that energy will come from renewable, green sources. But the fact that the market right now is relatively small for green energy sources—not to mention related green products—shouldn't be disconcerting to anyone. Rather, it should be seen as a huge opportunity. Chapter 2 features more about the market potential for green energy generation and products.

Energy Security: The New Cold War

If there were ever a more politically charged commodity than oil, then I would like someone smarter than I to explain it.

Oil is at the fulcrum of what is, in my opinion, the great global conflict of our lifetime.

I think most people fail to really understand the significance of energy security issues, or what I call the new cold war. This new cold war isn't a war in the traditional sense, although we have entered into armed conflict many times to a significant degree because of oil issues (Gulf Wars I and II are the most recent). This new cold war is, in fact, an energy war. It's an oil war.

Those of you old enough to remember the cold war climate in the 1950s, '60s, '70s, and '80s will understand the nature of this conflict best. This was the constant presence of tension between the communist Eastern bloc states and the capitalist West over who would essentially be the dominant world influence. This conflict went away a couple of decades ago, and the reason why was that the West won. The Soviet evil empire crumbled, and with it the communist influence on eastern Europe and other satellite states.

In the case of the cold war, we were fighting against a specific opponent, and it was a war that you could actually win. Unfortunately, I think when it comes to the current battle for global energy resources, we are in a battle for control that we really cannot win. It's nearly physically impossible—barring a U.S. invasion of the rest of the world, which I'm fairly sure is not going to happen—for Western military power to literally take control over the world's oil supplies.

The unfortunate fact for most of the free world is that the greatest natural resource the world has ever known is tied up largely in countries that at best tolerate the West as trading partners, and at worst think of the West as the Great Satan that deserves to be struck down by the vengeful wrath of Allah. With peak oil either already upon us or only a few years into the future, the implication for oil prices is profound.

The Usual Suspects

Iran, Iraq, Saudi Arabia, Russia, China, Venezuela, and Nigeria: This is the short list of usual suspects when it comes to countries in control of the world's oil supplies. With the possible exception of Iraq and the potential for a U.S. friendly government in that newborn and still unstable country, the primary oil-rich nations here each have an axe to grind with the West.

Sure, we've had friendly relations with Russia and China since the end of the cold war, but both countries still have a vested interest in remaining strong military and economic powers that can influence their respective regions as well as the rest of the world. One way to exert this influence is to control as much of the world's oil as possible.

Over the past several years, China has gone on a global oil grab that's seen the country secure long-term contracts for both oil and natural gas. This isn't as much of a bellicose move against the world as it is a need to supply their young and exponentially growing industrialized economy with the energy it needs to continue expanding.

This oil grab from China might be necessary for that country's future prosperity, but its effect on the rest of the globe is to lift the price of a barrel of crude. The higher demand, coupled with a restricted peak oil supply, means higher energy costs. It's just that simple.

Another front in this new cold war over oil is Russia. The former Soviet Union may not look at the West with the kind of hostile intent it once had, but the country still sees itself as a world power. The difference is that now, the Russian government's weapons have become their oil and natural gas reserves.

Perhaps the two biggest thorns in the side of the West come from Iran and Venezuela. Both of these countries' respective leaders, the fanatical but cunning Mahmoud Ahmadinejad and the boisterous and belligerent Hugo Chavez, have at their disposal a large portion of the world's crude oil supplies. These are men who have philosophical as well as strategic interests at odds with the West, and their hold on oil supplies is just one more reason energy security is one of the Big Three catalysts driving our push toward green energy sources.

You see, the key here is that if we can wean ourselves off of petroleum sources that exist in hostile territories, we can increase our energy security and decrease our vulnerability to energy supply disruptions. One way to do this is to have more homegrown renewable energy sources.

The less we have to rely on others for our energy needs, the less we have to fear, and the more energy secure we will be.

Carbon Concerns

Now we've come to what I think is perhaps the biggest social awareness driver fueling the green movement, and that is the growing concern over the deleterious effects on the planet of carbon emissions. Of course, the corollary to this concern is global climate change, or global warming, which is now a concept burned into the minds of just about everyone on the planet.

We all know about former Vice President Al Gore and his book and documentary film, *An Inconvenient Truth.* Mr. Gore garnered an Academy Award for the film and won a Nobel Peace Prize—along with the Intergovernmental Panel on Climate Change—for their part in bringing the prospective dangers of global warming to light. But just how much carbon is emitted by the world, and how much more carbon will an energy rich world spew out in the next several decades? For those projections let's return to data from the Energy Information Administration (2007).

According to the EIA, world carbon dioxide emissions are projected to rise from 26.9 billion metric tons in 2004 to 33.9 billion metric tons in 2015 and 42.9 billion metric tons in 2030.

That's a lot of carbon, so it's no wonder that it is such a big concern.

And where is that carbon coming from? Well, in 2004 CO_2 emissions from petroleum and other liquids' combustion made up about 40 percent of total emissions. By 2030 its share is projected to be 36 percent. Carbon dioxide emissions from natural gas combustion accounted for 20 percent of the 2004 total. That share is projected to rise to 21 percent in 2030. Coal's share in 2004 was 39 percent, but its share of total CO_2 is projected to increase to 43 percent by 2030.

Figure 1.4 shows the projected totals of CO_2 emissions by fuel type up through 2030. As the growth of Chindia occurs over the next few decades, it will become a huge contributor to global CO_2 emissions. In 2004 China and India combined for 22 percent of world emissions. The EIA predicts that by 2030, carbon dioxide emissions from China and India combined are projected to account for 31 percent percent of total world emissions.

Finally, what is the rate of growth of these carbon emissions?

The EIA projects that world energy-related carbon dioxide emissions will grow by an average of 1.8 percent per year from 2004 to 2030. For the OECD countries, total emissions are projected to average 0.8 percent annual growth. For non-OECD countries, total carbon dioxide emissions are projected to average 2.6 percent annual growth. This emissions extravaganza is lead by China, where that country's emissions are expected to rise by 3.4 percent annually

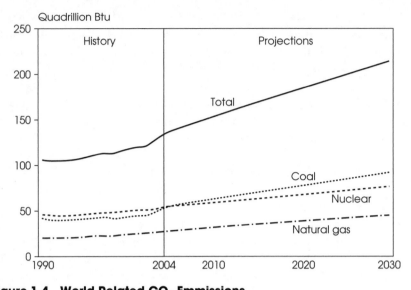

Figure 1.4   World Related CO₂ Emmissions

Source: Figure 78 from EIA, *International Energy Outlook 2007* (Washington, D.C.: U.S. Department of Energy, May 2007), p. 73.

from 2004 to 2030. The bottom line here is that CO$_2$ emissions will continue growing and that means a greater chance of global warming and its potentially devastating environmental effects.

Now this book does not take on the scientific debate concerning global climate change. What is important to understand for you, the individual investor, is that there is a consensus in the scientific community that anthropogenic (human-caused) carbon emissions are causing a rise in greenhouse gases, and this is causing a rise in global temperatures.

To combat this condition, something has to be done, and it has to be done soon. Why? Well, because the atmosphere has a long memory. It effectively accumulates all CO$_2$ and emissions we put up every year, and that's why CO$_2$ concentrations rise over time.

What is most disturbing about this long atmospheric memory is that even if you manage to make a modest change in emissions, it would only delay and not prevent the concentration from crossing what scientists suspect are dangerous CO$_2$ thresholds.

Some scientists argue that we have to make drastic reductions in emissions by the end of the century if we have any hope of stabilizing CO$_2$ concentrations. One way to reduce emissions is to be green, and fortunately for you, the investor, this is your ticket to making green. You see, the world will need technological solutions to assuage its carbon concerns. It is going to need new ideas, new products, new financing, new research, new brain power—in fact, it's going to need a whole new way of looking at the world.

We've already started to look through green-colored glasses, and that's what's so great about this whole field. That new need for green will make you green, if you know where to find it.

Mandating Growth

CREATING GREENER PASTURES

A change in the weather is sufficient to recreate the world and ourselves.

—Marcel Proust

Now that you know the Big Three demand drivers that are pushing us toward a greener path, it's time to look specifically at how the world is going about the process of becoming green.

There are several major factors leading the world toward its green transformation. The first push for green is coming from society at large through government action. Using its power of the purse and ability to enact and enforce laws and regulations to shape—some say distort—business decisions in favor of certain industries and technologies, governments around the world are creating the right conditions for green investment and research.

In many cases, that green investment comes in the form of direct tax dollars. Other times it takes the form of laws, incentives, subsidies, and mandates. Whatever form they take, action by governments is working to help mandate growth in virtually every green area pertinent to investors.

The governmental push for all things green has also put the economics of green in the favorable column for those who control the flow of capital. Venture capital investment in green market sectors has exploded in the twenty-first century, and that money has already found its way back to individual investors positioned in the companies benefiting most from the green explosion.

Finally, the growth mandated by a combination of government action and capital influx in green industries is creating a mega-sized profit opportunity in what is still an incredibly young industry.

In this chapter we'll take a broad look at governmental role in all things green, and we'll take a look at the data showing just how much money is going to new green ventures. We'll finish up the discussion by looking at just how potentially huge the green market could be in the coming years.

Green Public Policy

In December 2007, President George W. Bush signed the Energy Independence and Security Act (EISA) of 2007, a series of federal laws designed to improve motor vehicle fuel economy and increase alternative fuel usage.

EISA may increase the use of renewable fuels by 500 percent if fuel producers meet its requirement to supply at least 36 billion gallons of renewable fuel in the year 2022. The vehicle fuel economy mandate in EISA specifies a national mandatory fuel economy standard of 35 miles per gallon by 2020, which will save billions of gallons of fuel and increase efficiency by 40 percent.

EISA also mandates a phasing out of the use of incandescent light bulbs by 2014, a move thought to improve lighting efficiency by more than 70 percent by 2020. Other notable provisions in the new law include many new energy efficiency standards for appliances as well as new energy consumption reduction standards for all federal government facilities.

EISA is a great example of how governmental policy attempts to influence the green movement. By codifying things such as fuel efficiency standards and the elimination of certain products, government can really set industries and consumers on a greener path. Of course, EISA is just one of many, many government programs being implemented all over the globe that target green-related issues.

So, what other forms do these government programs take? Well, perhaps the biggest way government policy helps direct society toward being green is through subsidies and tax breaks. These tax breaks are too numerous to go through here, but each of the green sectors covered in this book have benefited from capital grants, investment tax credits, production tax credits, sales tax credits, and a host of other tax-related incentives.

Renewable portfolio standards (RPS) for utility companies—these require a certain amount of their total power generation be from renewable energy (solar, wind, geothermal, etc.)—helps force a market for renewables where one may not have existed otherwise. Along with utility company RPS is what's called *feed-in tariffs*. These establish a guaranteed price for power generated from renewables. By setting such a price, utility companies are assured of a return on the capital laid out to create renewable power.

Other government programs include low-interest loans and loan guarantees; greener building codes; efficiency standards for autos, appliances, and lighting; and biofuel usage requirements.

Using this variety of tools at its disposal, governments have really begun to enter into the promotion of all things green. Some critics have accused these actions as merely public relations moves, but whether it's for PR purposes or for any other reason, the fact that governments are glomming on to the green agenda worldwide is undeniable.

Yet another way governments are playing a key role in the green wave is in making renewable energy targets. These targets require a certain amount of a nation's energy come from green sources. Renewable energy targets are not *how* governments influence the green picture. Rather, they represent the will of the people to have a certain overriding goal achieved.

Leading the way on this front are the 25 European Union countries, all of which have undertaken at least some level of renewable targets. On average, the EU's goal is to have about 20 percent of its energy coming from renewables by 2010. The United States doesn't have a federal renewable energy target, but to date many states have implemented their own. States such as California, Texas, Nevada, and Hawaii are leading the way forward when it comes to being green, and that is yet another piece of great news for companies that make the products and technologies necessary to get us up to green speed.

Perhaps the biggest government factor in getting us green has to do with carbon emissions regulation. Here the Kyoto Protocol comes to mind as the biggest worldwide attempt to curb greenhouse gases and to thwart the potentially pernicious effects of global warming.

The Kyoto Protocol was created in 1997, and the international treaty was signed on to by more than 160 countries. The treaty is an agreement to essentially limit the CO_2 emissions by about 5 percent from 1990 to 2012. The big rub here with Kyoto is that three of the biggest CO_2-emitting nations—China, India, and the United States—are not operating under the mandates of the treaty.

Certainly, a worldwide commitment to curbing CO_2 emissions would indeed be a huge driving force in the world's quest to be green. But given the current political opposition from the Bush administration toward Kyoto standards, the likelihood of the United States signing on to any kind of carbon emissions caps is unlikely.

In Chapter 1 we saw that the developing world—led by Chindia—is going to require greater and greater energy to meet their growing demand. That energy will come primarily from fossil fuels, and that means more CO_2 emissions from the region. Given this situation, it is hard to see Chindia volunteering for some kind of CO_2 emissions cap that would likely stifle their economic ascendancy.

In my opinion, there isn't likely to be any progress made in the United States on this issue until well into 2009, after a new president moves into the White House. But even with a new administration in place—and even if that administration is for curbing CO_2—a big push toward heavy CO_2 reduction right out of the gate is unlikely. The wheels of government grind slowly, especially when it comes to signing global regulatory treaties.

Mo' Money, Mo' Growth

Capital is always the key to any growth equation. Be it the Internet boom of the 1990s or the real estate boom in the mid-2000s, the key ingredient driving expansion is always money.

Now when it comes to the green wave, capital investment is growing like a proverbial weed. According to the research group Clean Edge, U.S.-based venture capital investments in energy technologies more than quadrupled from $599 million in 2000 to $2.7 billion in 2007 (Makower, Pernick, and Wilder, 2008). As a percentage of total venture capital, energy technology increased from well under 1 percent in 2000 to over 9 percent in 2007. Between 2006 and 2007, venture capital investments in the U.S. clean energy space increased by more than 70 percent.

New Energy Finance estimates that worldwide, total global investment in all clean-energy sectors surged from $92.6 billion in 2006 to $148.4 billion in 2007. That's a 60 percent increase in total clean-energy investment in just one year. These figures, by the way, do include not just venture capital, but capital raised in public markets via initial public offerings; project financing; asset financing; and government and corporate research, development and deployment.

Remember that old adage "follow the money"? Well, that's exactly what we are doing here, and there is no doubt that in recent years, the money is following all things green. And while nearly $150 billion in one year is a big wad of cash to throw around, I think the best is yet to come. In my opinion we'll look on this figure as just a drop in the overall green bucket. Why? Well, given the reasons outlined in Chapter 1, and the governmental policy we've seen here in Chapter 2, you can conclude that the race to get green will continue running for quite a while.

It seems like my thesis for greater and greater capital investment is also shared by the very smart folks at the International Energy Agency (2007). According to their latest estimates, $16 trillion needs to be invested by 2030 to meet the growth in projected demand for electricity and fuel worldwide. That's about $600 billion a year. I suspect much of that will go into green energy production, and that means growth in the space is going to be with us for a very long time.

The Green Capital Boom

As it is known to do, the private sector responds enthusiastically to an opportunity to make a big return on investment. It is no surprise, then, that many of the biggest venture capitalists who financed promising Internet companies in the 1990s are now financing promising alternative energy start-ups.

The big green capital boom would likely not happen without a mix of government incentives, mandates, and subsidies, the likes of which we've already discussed. In fact, booms happen precisely when the smart money places its bets on the hottest areas in the market. Now some may say that the government is encouraging a green bubble by implementing favorable policies toward being green. And while this may be true, I know quite a few multimillionaires that were created by investing in the Internet and real estate bubbles. The key for the investor is to "know how to pick 'em"—which is covered in the chapters to come.

One thing to keep in mind here is that government, through various industrial policies, has a long history of influencing private sector capital toward investing in new technologies. Congress commissioned the first telegraph line in the 1840s and gave railroads land to build rail networks. The government also financed the research that led to the creation of the Internet.

Now we all know the old joke about Al Gore and his claim to have invented the Internet. The former VP did not actually make this claim—he meant that he had been an early proponent—but such is the nature of damaging quotations. Now, Al Gore is back in a big way, not only with his work as a global climate change activist, but also as a consultant to one of the most prestigious venture capital (VC) firms around—Kleiner Perkins Caufield & Byers.

In November 2007, the former vice president signed on with Silicon Valley's VC elite. Given Mr. Gore's bona fides on the green front, the move by the ultra-smart folks at Kleiner Perkins will boost the firm's profile as a leader in the green investing space.

The hiring of Gore is significant not because of what he can bring to the table for Kleiner Perkins—although I am sure the Nobel Prize winner's prominence will contribute to their goals. Rather, I think it is significant in terms of a tipping point in the wider awareness of the green capital boom.

What you have to realize is that it was just a few years ago that investments in green industries were largely just small blips in the overall venture capital radar. Most VC firms and Wall Street investment houses didn't pay much attention to green because it wasn't really big enough to pay attention. Today, that perception has been annihilated, and greening of the capital markets has caught on in a big way.

The VC View

In March 2008, a panel of venture capitalists gathered at the Globe 2008 business conference in Vancouver, Canada. Conferences like this one have become ubiquitous in recent years—I know, I have attended quite a few—and they speak to the overwhelming desire capital has to find big opportunities in green technology. One thing to keep in mind here is that these opportunities, though very real and potentially very lucrative, could take longer to come to fruition than other VC-driven sectors like the Internet or semiconductors.

The reason for this longer VC waiting period has to do with the capital-intensive nature of green technology sectors. Think about how difficult it would be to reinvent the infrastructure that was put in place to support the internal combustion engine or the coal-driven power grid, and you can start to see why the scope and size of green technology industries is so massive.

Another issue affecting capital influx into green is the many options out there. To be sure, choice is a great thing, yet the very broad nature of green and its myriad sectors and subsectors—many of which you will learn about in this book—makes allocating always-scarce capital resources toward the greatest return on capital.

If you think this task is difficult for venture capitalists, and believe me it is, then it stands to reason that the task of picking the best of the best investments as an individual investor will be even harder. But if I do my job properly, you'll learn how to use this book to help you make the right decisions about how to make green.

Making Real Money

A billion here, a billion there; pretty soon you are talking about real money.

According to the research group Clean Edge, in its *Clean Energy Trends 2008* report, the alternative energy business is starting to make real money. Worldwide sales for companies specializing in biofuels, wind farms, solar panels, and fuel cells grew 40 percent in 2007 to reach $77.3 billion.

That's real money my friends, especially considering the fact that in 2007 there were many green start-up firms that didn't even have a product to sell. I remember back in the Internet boom days, when revenues were hardly even considered an important factor when investing in the space. Today, we know revenues matter in even the hottest new industry, and the Clean Edge data proves that although green industries are still largely in their infancy, they can still deliver on what venture capitalists and Wall Street love to see—revenues.

Broken down by industry, Clean Edge found revenue in the wind power industry jumped 68 percent in 2007 to reach $30.1 billion as new wind farms sprouted across the United States and China. Sales of ethanol and biodiesel, together, grew about 24 percent to hit $25.4 billion. Solar photovoltaic sales grew 30 percent, totaling $20.3 billion.

The real beauty of those numbers lies in the fact that compared to the traditional energy business, they're minuscule. To get a sense of scale one need not look any further than the oil industry, which many alternative energy enthusiasts would love to replace. Exxon Mobil, the world's largest international oil company, reported $404.5 billion in sales in 2007. That's more than five times the entire alternative energy industry combined. Mind you, this is just one—albeit very, very large—energy company.

Why do I refer to this situation as "real beauty"? Because the relatively tiny green energy market right now just means there's more room to grow green. I call it *green headroom,* meaning there is vast potential for more and more revenue growth, and more opportunity for green technologies to take a bite out of the overwhelming domination of traditional energy sources.

By now I think that an airtight case has been made as to the influence government policy and capital has on green industries. The world's venture capitalists have embraced green technology in a big way, and I expect more and more money to pour into the multiple market segments striving to make the world greener.

But before we move on and look at each green sector individually, I want to impart a few final thoughts on the big picture. What I think is really important to grasp about energy issues and green technology's role in solving the world's challenges is the tremendous scale involved when dealing with these issues. The sheer size and enormity of both the opportunity and the challenge is unlike anything the world has ever seen.

Furthermore, when it comes to being green, government policy and regulation matters. Like it or not, there are very few aspects of the green market that aren't heavily regulated, incentivized, subsidized, or just plain controlled by government policy. Add to this the challenge of energy security and possible global destruction from CO_2 emissions and you've got yourself a real intoxicating cocktail bound to give the world a hangover for many years—*if* we don't continue down the green path.

Finally, the psychic benefit of this whole thing is that by investing in green companies and industries, you are doing something not only for yourself, but for the entire salvation of planet Earth. I've often said that investing in green companies allows you not only to make a fortune, but also to save the world. Hey, I can't think of anything better than helping others and getting rich at the same time. That, in my view, is the best job around. Now with those thoughts in mind, let's take a look at our first green sector—transportation.

CHAPTER

Waving The Green Flag

CLEAN TRANSPORTATION

*Greater than the tread of mighty armies is an idea
whose time has come.*

—Victor Hugo

I love the smell of ethanol in the morning.

The morning I refer to is April 19, 2008, when I was trackside at the longest-running major automotive street race held in North America—the 34th annual Toyota Grand Prix of Long Beach. This year's Grand Prix featured the raw engine power of the Corvette Racing team, whose 600-plus horsepower engines run exclusively on cellulosic E85 ethanol (85 percent ethanol, 15 percent gasoline). This high-octane, renewable alternative fuel is made from waste wood and switchgrass.

Hey, when one of America's premier sports car racing teams pops the champagne in victory lane while simultaneously being greener than its competition, you know you've got the makings of a green future for the transportation sector. But Corvette Racing wasn't the only green transportation featured over the three-day Grand Prix weekend.

The event, the Green Power Prix-View, drew nearly 200,000 fans and was a veritable celebration of Southern California car culture. This year, however, a very real feeling of change ran through the participants that their culture is undergoing a profound change—and that change is the greening of the transportation industry.

The organizers of the Green Power Prix-View showcased for the first time a green lifestyle and alternative energy expo that took up approximately 30,000 square feet of space at the Long Beach Convention Center. Vehicles ranging from hydrogen-powered cars, electric cars, hybrid-electric cars, flex-fuel cars, electric motorbikes, even solar-powered vehicles were all on display. Perhaps the best-known of all green vehicles, the Toyota Prius, also served as the pace car for the many races held over the three-day weekend.

The greening of the Long Beach Grand Prix in 2008 speaks volumes about the current mood in the transportation industry. I remember just a few years ago when fuel economy and pollution concerns took a backseat (pardon the pun) to the bigger-is-better sport utility vehicle (SUV) craze. Giant-sized vehicles like the Chevrolet Suburban, the Ford Excursion, and the Hummer H2 dominated the car culture crowd back then, and while those vehicles are still very popular, they are nowhere near as talked about nor as desirable to own as they once were.

The Zeitgeist in the personal transportation sector is indeed changing and this is reflected in the many new green vehicle models being offered by established auto industry giants. But it's not just the big boys getting into the green vehicle game. There are a slew of new start-up companies plunging headfirst into what has traditionally been one of the toughest industries to break into, and one with very significant barriers to entry.

So, what are the various options available to those who want to be green in the way they get around town? More importantly, what are the best choices for investors when it comes to profiting from this new green Zeitgeist? Let's take a closer look at the problems facing the transportation industry, and the solutions that are either available to your garage right now, or that could be parked in your garage soon.

Driving Along in My Automobile

It's just a fact of reality that the richer a society gets, the more mobile it gets. With more economic freedom comes greater freedom to get out and explore the world around you. That's certainly been true throughout history, and well before there was ever anything conceived of like the internal combustion engine.

Right now there are approximately 800 million motor vehicles currently operating around the world. Now, I doubt it will come as much of a surprise to you that the United States accounts for a big chunk of that. Anyone who has ever traversed a big-city American freeway can attest to the fact that there are lots and lots of vehicles out there. I've seen the number pegged at somewhere around 250 million motor vehicles in the United States, but I wouldn't be surprised if both the total number of vehicles worldwide and the number in the United States are higher.

But the real problem—or challenge as I see it—is how will the world deal with the surge of consumers in Chindia and the carbon emissions created by an a new class of consumers finally wealthy enough to afford the luxury of mobility? When you consider that the internal combustion engine, the lifeblood of the transportation industry for over 100 years, has that pesky little side effect of sending a lot of CO_2 and other greenhouse gases into the atmosphere, you realize that any major proliferation in cars and trucks worldwide is a serious issue.

If demand for cars and trucks were to continue even at a moderate pace, by 2020 there could be as many as 1 billion (yes, billion with a "b") internal combustion engines burning up the roads and sending greenhouse gases into the earth's atmosphere. According to the Energy Information Administration, 43 percent of the world's increase in oil demand from 2003 to 2030 will come from China, India, and the developing countries in Asia. That explosive new oil demand is going to go, in large part, directly into the tanks of the millions of new automobile owners in the developing world.

I explained this situation to one of my friends in the academic world, and he told me quite candidly that what I had here was a "problem." Well, in the business community, we don't see things so much in terms of problems; we prefer to call situations like these challenges or opportunities.

A Green Way Forward

The Michelin tire company is best known for its corpulent, white-bodied mascot, whose official name is "Bibendum," although most people know him simply as the "Michelin Man." But I want to put a little twist on Michelin's actual motto, "A better way forward." I think that in terms of the future of transportation, the world's motto should be "A greener way forward."

How do we get from CO_2 emitting engines to a cleaner, greener way forward? The first step is knowing our options. Of course, the first option is to make vehicles more fuel efficient. That's being done via legislation such as the new fuel economy standards outlined in the Energy Independence and Security Act (EISA) of 2007 discussed in Chapter 2. But just increasing fuel economy standards for internal combustion engines won't really get us on the path to a green way forward.

To make a substantial dent in the reliance on petroleum-powered vehicles, many automakers and auto technology firms are developing a better, greener vehicular mousetrap. Case in point is the aforementioned Michelin tire company, which holds an annual event called Challenge Bibendum.

In October 1998 the company organized a birthday celebration to mark the centenary of the Bibendum mascot. The celebration took the form of a road rally for advanced technology vehicles from Clermont-Ferrand to Paris designed to demonstrate that the automotive industry was already working towards what the company calls "sustainable mobility."

A decade later, the Challenge Bibendum has achieved world-wide recognition as the premier event in promoting sustainable road mobility. It's an event where industry, policy makers, academia, and the media can review the latest technologies, debate policies, and share their visions about how to make a greener way forward.

The Challenge Bibendum has been a showcase for many alternative fuel and hybrid electric vehicles over the years, but just what are these vehicles and how do they work? Let's take a closer look at the current crop of greener transportation options.

The Hybrid Theory

The most familiar form of green transport available to consumers right now is the *hybrid electric vehicle,* or HEV, which is also assisted by a gasoline-powered internal combustion engine, hence the word "hybrid." When people think of green vehicles, these are usually the first types that come to mind. There were over 250,000 HEVs sold in 2006, and while this represents only about 1.5 percent of the total number of autos sold that year, predictions for huge growth in the industry are stunning.

Global demand for hybrid electric vehicles is estimated to grow by about 20 percent annually through 2010. Market share gains for these fuel-efficient vehicles will be driven by high fuel prices, increased emissions regulations, and lowering HEV cost disparities. The United States, Western Europe, and Japan will remain the top markets, but China is going to catching up fast.

The basic premise of a hybrid electric vehicle is that it is powered by both a traditional internal combustion petroleum-burning engine and an electric motor. The electric motor is powered by batteries, which are charged either by the engine or by what's called *regenerative braking*. This process occurs as the electric motor applies resistance to the vehicle's drive train, which causes the wheels to slow down. In return, the energy from the wheels turns the motor, which functions as a generator, converting energy normally wasted during coasting and braking into electricity. That electricity is then stored in a battery until it's needed by the electric motor. If you think this is an ingenious idea, wait until you read about some of the other technological solutions brewing in this industry (more on that in a moment).

The advantages of HEVs are that they improve fuel economy and they reduce CO_2 and other pollution emissions. The Holy Grail of greener transport is to get us where we want to go, without adding any harmful elements to our environment, and although HEVs are a good start, they are just that—a start.

In terms of the companies manufacturing HEVs, it reads like a Who's Who of automotive giants. Toyota Motor Corp. (NYSE: TM) is by far the leader in HEV sales with its Prius model HEV. In fact, Toyota is on the cusp of taking over the top spot as the world's leading automaker from perennial industry dominator General Motors (NYSE: GM), and much of Toyota's appeal can be attributed to both the quality of its products and the innovative, fuel-saving technology embedded into vehicles like the Prius.

In addition to the Prius, Toyota also offers hybrid versions of their ultra-popular Camry and the Highlander. Honda Motor Co. (NYSE: HMC) is the second-closest competitor to Toyota in terms of hybrid vehicles sales. The company's Insight and hybrid Civic models, while not nearly as popular as Toyota's hybrid offerings, are still racking up respectable sales worldwide. Not to be outdone, American car manufacturers have stepped up to the starting grid with their own HEV offerings. Ford Motor Co. (NYSE: F) now offers a hybrid version of its Escape, which the company calls a "guilt-free SUV." General Motors now sells hybrid Chevrolet and GMC SUVs, as well as hybrid Saturn models. In the coming years, look for a plethora of new HEV models from these not only the aforementioned automakers, but from nearly every major automaker.

The downside for the consumer in owning an HEV is up-front cost. Depending on the model, a hybrid cost about $5,000 more than a comparable conventional vehicle. This cost is largely off-set by federal tax credits given to HEV buyers, and by the fact that HEVs average about twice the fuel economy of their conventional gasoline engine counterparts. As fuel prices continue rising, the national average per gallon in April 2008 was nearly $4, the allure of a vehicle that gets twice as many miles per gallon is destined to become more and more popular.

As the trend toward a greener way forward plays out, expect to see HEV sales play a bigger and bigger part in terms of total auto sales in the United States and worldwide. The emergence and now virtual mainstreaming of HEVs is what I pointed out to my academic friend as one way that industry is overcoming the challenges associated with reducing CO_2 emissions provider greener transportation to a mobile world.

Plug In and Fire Up the Engine

HEVs are the current iteration of greener transport, but the next step in greener mobility will undoubtedly be the *plug-in hybrid electric vehicle,* also known as PHEV. The plug-in hybrid is different from the HEV in two fundamental ways. First, the PHEV's primary source of power is an electric battery. Yes, it does have an internal combustion engine, but that engine is used mainly as a way to boost horsepower when needed. The second major difference is in the technology used in the PHEV batteries.

Unlike HEV, PHEV vehicle batteries can be recharged simply by plugging them into an ordinary 110-volt electrical outlet. With PHEVs, you can use the power you already get from your utility company to essentially fill your tank. The promise of plug-in vehicles is truly revolutionary. The widespread use of such technology to green our primary mode of personal transportation would likely take a big bite out of our dependence on foreign oil. It would also mean a significant reduction in CO_2 and other greenhouse gases.

From a consumer standpoint, PHEV use would mean a huge reduction in vehicle operation costs. Because PHEVs will get much better fuel mileage than HEVs—some estimates are between 100 and 150 miles per gallon—the consumer would be able to go a lot further with a lot less out-of-pocket monetary green.

What's the problem with mass adoption of PHEVs? Why aren't automakers rushing to get these vehicles to the market pronto? Actually, many automakers are trying to get a viable PHEV vehicle mass produced. The problem with mass production of PHEVs at this stage is battery technology. Lithium batteries are currently the main technology for PHEVs. And yes, that's the same lithium battery technology used in my favorite electronic gadgets such as cell phones. But this technology has the unfortunate side effect of creating a lot of heat. The tendency to overheat can be a danger, especially in a big mechanical device like an automobile.

I think once the technical challenges in developing the next iteration of lithium batteries is largely overcome, including the ability to reduce the overall cost of this sophisticated battery type, the floodgates are going to open up big time in terms of the move to PHEVs. I don't know about you, but I would love to just plug my vehicle into an outlet in my garage and basically be set to go about my business. Sure, with a PHEV I may still have to visit the gas station, but definitely not as frequently—and it would definitely cost me a lot less overall.

EV All the Way

Now if HEVs are good, and PHEVs are even better, what about a 100 percent electric vehicle? Wouldn't that be the ultimate solution to the challenges of creating a green way forward? The answer, of course, is yes, but are we anywhere close? The answer is a most definite yes.

Electric vehicles, or EVs, are already past the drawing board stage. One company, the privately held Tesla Motors, has developed a downright cool-looking all-electric vehicle designed around the very sporty Lotus Elise chassis. The best part of the Tesla Roadster sports car model—at least for a car guy like me—is the vehicle's performance stats. The Tesla Roadster can go from 0 to 60 miles per hour in under four seconds. That's considered supercar performance, and the most impressive thing about the car is that it gets you there that quickly entirely via the power of lithium batteries—about 6,300 of the small batteries to be exact. Oh, and the other great thing about the Tesla Roadster is you never, ever have to stop at a gas station again—unless, of course, you get hungry during your weekend drive and want to fuel your body up on snacks.

Now the Tesla Roadster isn't aimed at a really big mass market just yet. The car will carry a hefty price tag of over $90,000, but already the company has sold out the first planned run of 250 vehicles. According to Tesla, the equivalent mileage on the Roadster will be about 135 miles per gallon. Of course, there are no "gallons" with EVs, and that's the real beauty of the Tesla, and the future role of EVs in greening our transportation.

Tesla Motors is a great example of what entrepreneurs can do when they think in unconventional ways. And while Tesla has seen a lot of positive publicity in the automotive trade magazines and even in the mainstream press, the company is by no means the only green transportation start-up out there.

By my count there are nearly 20 new EV startups (including Tesla) on their way to taking the nation's highways by storm. There's AC Propulsion, Aptera, Brammo, Fisker Automotive, Lightning, Miles Automotive, Myers Motors, Phoenix Motorcars, Porteon, REVA Electric Car, Think, Ultramotor, Vectrix, Venture Vehicles, Wrightspeed, Zap, Zenn Motors, and Zero Motorcycles.

This list is not comprehensive. I expect to see many more companies engaged in EV research and development, and in building a greener horse and buggy. Of course, don't ever forget about the major automakers. These guys have the money, market share, and distribution network that could overwhelm any start up EV firm if they really wanted to commit to mass sales of EVs.

Whenever I bring up EVs with friends, they always ask what I think are very good questions. Because EVs don't burn gasoline, what about the electric power used to recharge the batteries? Doesn't that power come from the power grid, and doesn't generating power through either a coal-burning or natural gas–burning power plant contribute to the CO_2 and greenhouse gas emissions? The answer is yes, but the extra CO_2 and other greenhouse gas emissions generated from powering up PHEVs and HEVs would be significantly less than what comes out of our cars' tailpipes. And, if you were getting your home power from sources such as solar or wind, you would really be going green. By some estimates, overall greenhouse gas emissions would be reduced anywhere from 20 percent to 60 percent by running EV cars off the electric grid. That's a big reduction, and it's one the world will soon strive for in its quest for greener mobility.

How Do We Make Money?

Here's the tricky part of the green transportation equation. You see, it's one thing to wax eloquent about how cool the Tesla Roadster is going to be, but it's another thing for investors to actually make money from publicly traded stocks in the green transportation sector.

Right now your options are somewhat limited in this field. As a general guideline, however, you'll want to choose automaker stocks such as Toyota and Honda over GM and Ford. If you had placed your bet on these two Japanese auto giants in recent years, and stayed away from GM and Ford, you'd have a lot more green of the monetary variety in your portfolio. But investing in automakers is not where the real green will be made.

Building a better, more efficient battery is where the real money is to be made. Companies—and their investors—that solve the battery limitations that prevent the wider acceptance and utility of electric vehicles with new and better technology will be the real winners in the green transportation wave. Think of companies supplying new and better battery technology to the auto industry in the same way as companies who supplied modems and software to get computers onto the Internet.

Who are the players in this industry? The companies described next are making big strides and are well positioned for growth going forward.

Energy Conversion Devices

You are going to hear a lot more about Energy Conversion Devices, or ECD Ovonics (Nasdaq: ENER). This company, which is described in more detail Chapter 4, is a big diversified player in many green-investing areas. When it comes to hybrid batteries, the company's subsidiary, Cobasys—a joint venture with Chevron Technology Ventures—is a prime player. Cobasys designs, manufactures and integrates advanced battery system solutions featuring *nickel-metal hydride* (NiMH) batteries for transportation markets, including HEVs, PHEVs, and EVs. Cobasys makes the NiMH battery system for GM's Saturn line of hybrid vehicles.

One thing I like about ECD Ovonics is the many battery technology patents the company holds. Because of its diversified intellectual property portfolio, this company is a great way to play the growth in the hybrid vehicle market.

Valence Technology

Valence Technology (Nasdaq: VLNC) is small battery maker that has developed a phosphate-based lithium-ion battery technology called *Saphion*. Saphion batteries are lighter and designed to store more energy than traditional lithium batteries. If the company's battery technology is successful, it will help make HEVs, PHEVs, and EVs safer, more reliable, and more affordable.

With phosphate to keep it from catching fire, the Saphion battery also is equipped with an advanced management system that monitors and enhances cell performance. The battery packs will be available in 12.8-volt and 19.2-volt modules, and the company says it hopes the batteries will be powering electric vehicle fleets in Europe soon.

Altair Nanotechnologies

Altair (Nasdaq: ALTI) is a nanotech firm chiefly concerned with building better, safer batteries. Its *NanoSafe* lithium ion batteries use a unique manufacturing process that incorporates nanoparticles of titanium dioxide and other ceramic oxide materials and compounds. This patented process results in very high-quality components such as Altair's nano-structured lithium-titanate anode material.

The company's Generation 2 batteries will be used to power the EVs manufactured by privately held Phoenix Motorcars. The all-electric *sport utility truck* (SUT) and *sport utility vehicle* (SUV) start-up has taken orders for fleet-ready vehicles for delivery in 2008 to premier fleet companies such as Pacific Gas & Electric and such California government entities as Santa Monica, San Bernardino County, Fresno County, and others.

Phoenix's zero-emission SUTs and SUVs can travel at freeway speeds while carrying four passengers and a full payload. The vehicles will have a driving range of over 100 miles. The best part here is that because of Altair Technologies advanced lithium-titanate batteries, Phoenix's vehicles can be recharged in less than 10 minutes. The battery pack is also very durable, boasting a life span of greater than 250,000 miles.

The Bleeding Edge

Now there are many other aspects of the green transportation sector we have not covered in this chapter. Bleeding edge technologies such as hydrogen fuel-cell vehicles (FCVs) have the potential to replace HEVs, PHEVs, and EVs, but their mass adoption is a long way away. Honda began leasing an FCV, the FCX Clarity, in summer 2008 in selected markets. Honda says the FCX Clarity can reach a top speed of 100 mph, and drivers can expect to get 270 miles from a full tank. The company says fuel economy is estimated at the equivalent of 68 miles per gallon of gasoline, based on the energy content of hydrogen versus gas.

Other technologies for a greener way forward include compressed air–powered vehicles, hydrogen-boosted engines and, of course, biofuels such as ethanol. We'll have much more to say about biomass and biofuels in Chapter 9.

Words of Caution

Before we move on to the next chapter, I want to add a few words of caution. Keep in mind that one of the main goals of this book is to teach you how to think about being green, and how to think about making green from the overriding trends in the clean energy and green lifestyle markets.

The discussion of companies here should not be construed as a direct recommendation to buy these securities. Rather, my comments on the stocks in each sector should be restricted to understanding how to find opportunities in the sector. Because of the ever-changing conditions in so many green market segments, there is no way a book can tell you which stocks will be the best to buy and/or stay away from at any given time.

The bottom line here is that what is a good green stock now could be a not-so-good green stock in the near future. Conversely, a green company that hasn't hit its stride may not even be included in the discussion here, but in the future it could be a tremendous opportunity for investors.

Finally, one reason I started this discussion with green transportation is that everyone is familiar with automobiles. Over the course of this book, you'll be introduced to some specific green market sectors that may not be as familiar to you as cars. This familiarity with an everyday product such as the car is a great way to show just how the green revolution may affect all of our everyday habits in the not-too-distant future.

While the opportunities for investors in the green transportation sector are not terribly numerous at this stage of the game, the topic of our next chapter is chock full of investable opportunities.

That topic is solar power, and now I think it's time to get out of our cars and soak up a little sun.

4

I Wanna Soak up the Sun!

HARNESSING THE PROFIT POWER OF SOLAR

Sunlight is painting.

—Nathaniel Hawthorne

In ancient Egyptian mythology, the sun god Ra used a solar barge to pass through the underworld each night so that he might rise in the morning. Human civilization has certainly come a long way in the five millennia since Ra. We now understand the intimate details of the nuclear fusion taking place moment by moment inside the sun's unimaginably hot interior. And now in the twenty-first century, we understand how to harness the sun's power to provide the energy that keeps our modern civilization thriving.

Indeed, the promise of the ultimate clean and renewable energy source is today a reality. The only questions now are: How long will it take for solar power to become cost competitive with traditional fossil fuel sources, and which companies will be best positioned to profit from the modern world's version of sun worship? This chapter will explore these and other crucial questions surrounding what could be the best green investing opportunity over the next several years and beyond.

Make no mistake about it, solar is no green fad. The economics of solar and the brainpower blueprint laid out by the related semiconductor sector make solar power generation one of the best hopes for a green-powered future. Along with the promise of solar come many myths and misconceptions. There are also many disadvantages to solar power as a primary energy producer. But there are a multitude of advantages to solar that, in my opinion, far outweigh its disadvantages and drawbacks. We'll go into the details of the minuses and pluses of solar, and we'll look at a few companies well positioned to bask in the sunshine.

Before we get into the details of investing in the solar space, we need to know the basics of how solar power works. Solar power, or to be more precise, solar photovoltaic (solar PV) power, is an ingenious use of sunlight to create a flow of electrons. Positive and negatively charged slices of silicon placed under a thin slice of glass, also known as a solar PV cell, serve as collectors for the sun's protons. As these protons beat down onto the PV cell, they knock neutrons off the silicon. The negatively charged free neutrons are then attracted to the silicon, but are trapped by the magnetic field that is formed from the opposing positive and negatively charged fields. Small wires attached to the silicon cells catch these neutrons and, when connected in a circuit, an electric current is formed.

The real work in this process is done by the solar PV cells. When these cells are assembled together in clusters, you get what most people are familiar with when they think of solar power—those glistening black rooftop fixtures known as *solar panels*. Given enough solar panels—and, of course, the requisite raw material sent down from the heavens by the sun god Ra—a substantial current can be generated. With the help of an inverter to change the direct current captured by the solar cells to an alternating current, the electricity can be used to power up any electronic device we want it to.

The best part about solar power—other than the ability to make green from investing in the best companies in the sector—is that the "fuel" from the sun is virtually a never-ending resource. Sure, the sun will eventually run out of the fuel it uses in a few million years, but I suspect your investment outlook is just a tad bit shorter than that.

The other great thing about solar is that it uses something nearly everyone is intimately familiar with—sand.

Sand and Sun, Not Just a Vacation Mantra

Yes, you read that right. Sand is the basic component of a solar PV cell. To be a bit more specific, that sand is actually silicon. This is the feedstock of the solar PV industry. This is where the so-called solar value chain begins. The process of making silicon starts by actually extracting the substance from the ground, then melting it at extremely high temperatures and treating it with siloxane gas, oxygen, and hydrochloric acid to raise purity to 99.9999 percent. The result is chunks of granulated pure silicon.

Step two is to transform that pure silicon into a mold to form ingots. These ingots, or big blocks of pure silicon, are then sectioned and literally sawed into very thin sections appropriately named wafers.

Step three is the actual creation of the aforementioned solar PV cells. The process involves a series of chemical and thermal treatments to introduce the electrical fields onto the cell. Etching of the wafer surface, the application of antireflective materials designed to increase light absorption, and the application of electrical contacts are all part of the solar cell creation process.

The fourth link in the solar value chain is the creation of solar modules. This is basically the connecting of solar cells so that they can function together as a unit. The fifth and final link in the chain is putting the construction of these modules into an array, which is then installed on a site such as the top of a building or in the middle of a solar collection area called a *solar farm*.

The reason I bring up this solar value chain is that throughout it there are companies leading the way and making money for shareholders. We'll name names in a moment, but first let's explore the advantages and disadvantages of using solar power to generate electricity.

When one of the main components in your power-generation model is raw material that's free of charge, that is to say, sunlight, you know you've got the makings of a nice start. This fuel that comes directly from Mother Nature doesn't require any kind of transportation, nor does it require any reliance on a supply that's located in remote desert, deep water, or otherwise hard to reach or politically challenging regions. With solar fuel, all we need to do is create the means by which to harvest the sun's photonic downpour.

Another advantage of solar is that it does not emit greenhouse gases and is effectively carbon neutral. Solar produces no wasteful by-products, which means that it is perhaps the greenest of all energy sources. Because solar cells are basically a moving part–free zone, solar PV cells and modules are very low maintenance. In fact, they can last decades with virtually no maintenance, which differs quite a bit from things like oil and gas drilling rigs or coal and natural gas generation plants.

Contrary to common belief, solar power works even if it's not a hot, sunny day. The sun's photons pummel the earth constantly, and just because it may be a gloomy day in the northern hemisphere, it doesn't mean that solar PV cells in that region aren't doing their thing. The reality is solar PV cells actually work best when ambient temperatures are moderate, say in the 70 degree range.

Other benefits of solar power include the end user's freedom from traditional power grid sources of energy. If there's a black-out, or if a utility company hikes power, it doesn't affect your solar PV cell operations. The cells just keep converting photons into electrical current, so you can light up your home, warehouse, or office building.

As for the disadvantages of solar, well there are a few, but "few" is the key word here. The first and most obvious disadvantage is that the sun shines only during the day. Therefore, solar power generation takes place only during daylight hours. This situation has an easy fix, however, as power storage systems such as batteries can be employed to capture and store the solar power.

The other disadvantage for solar is cost. Not only is there a substantial up front cost associated with solar power in the form of buying and installing the solar cells and modules needed to power a structure or large solar installation, but the actual cost per kilowatt-hour of solar is relatively expensive. According to consensus indus-try estimates, solar electric power costs about 20 to 25 cents per kilowatt-hour. That may not seem like a lot of money, but when you compare it to the average cost per kilowatt-hour of natural gas, which is about 7 cents, or to coal power, which is about 4 cents, you can see that solar is indeed quite expensive.

So why would anyone but the most hardcore green types actually spring for the additional cost of solar? There is a reason: End users don't have to pay the additional cost. That cost is largely made up via government incentives.

Costs and Incentives: Creating Sunny Choices

To be sure, the cost of solar energy is becoming more competi-tive each year even without a help from government incentives.

The declining price of solar is driven largely—as it is in most industries—by improved technology and efficiency. By some estimates, the cost of solar will fall to between 10 and 15 cents per kilowatt-hour by 2010. That may be optimistic, but even if we get anywhere close to this general cost area, solar's adoption rate is bound to go up significantly in the years to come (DOE, 2007).

According to the Department of Energy's Solar America Initiative (SAI) project, the cost of solar power generation is going to move steadily downward in the years ahead, possibly even becoming cost competitive with more traditional fossil fuel electricity generation by 2012. As greater energy demand from the developing world ratchets up fossil fuel costs, the cost advantages of traditional energy sources over solar are going to decline. Historically, the cost of solar has declined about 5 percent per year, and assuming the cost of solar continues declining at that rate, we are looking at a very attractive day in the sun for solar energy generation costs.

Still, the reality of the cost situation with solar is that it is not yet at parity with grid-generated electrical power. Solar-generated electricity cannot compete on a cost basis with coal- or natural gas–fired power plants, but the lack of sound economic decision making has never been the strong suit of government policy makers. And, in the case of solar, this lack of economic IQ is just fine with me.

The large up-front costs and relatively low utilization rates (remember, solar power generation is restricted to daylight hours when the sun is shining) for solar installations results in an installed production cost on the order of three to four times the retail price of traditional fossil fuel sources. Because of this price disparity, and because lawmakers and society at large want—and need—to go green with their power generation, government incentives are required to get people to make what would otherwise be an economically unsound power-generation choice.

It's been the massive footprint of solar incentives that's driven the growth of solar investment over the past decade, and by the looks of the current climate and tendency for policy makers around the globe to go green in bigger and bigger ways, solar's growth will continue to benefit from a cascade of incentives yet to come. In terms of the types of incentives operated in the solar sector, we have the feed-in tariff model most commonly employed in Europe, and the subsidy tax relief model found in the United States, both on the federal and state levels.

Hefty government support for solar projects in Germany, Spain, and many other European Union nations, along with support in Japan and even China is causing solar to grow at a very rapid pace worldwide. In the United States, the federal government provides special tax credits for renewable energy generation in general, and in particular solar PV installations. Tax credits on the order of 30 percent for residential and commercial photovoltaic systems have really assisted domestic solar growth, and with the climate in Washington green and likely to get even greener no matter who succeeds President Bush, federal support for solar should continue at least at its current rate.

But the feds aren't the only governmental entities getting in on the solar bonanza. State governments also have their funds in the solar pool, with over 40 states (as of late 2007) having some sort of solar incentive programs. The largest of the solar-friendly states is, predictably, the Golden State—eco-friendly California. The California Solar Initiative (CSI), which began in 2007, will provide $3.2 billion in rebates to both residential and commercial installations of solar systems. The overriding goal is to install 3,000 megawatts (MW) of solar modules in the state by 2016. That's about twice the current total demand for solar. Yes, this is ambitious in my view, but that kind of big thinking and big solar scale is what's going to help you make big bucks investing in the solar sector.

How big are we talking in terms of the solar market share and projected growth? Let's find out.

Let the Sunshine In

According to research firm Solarbuzz, world solar photovoltaic market installations reached a record high of 2,826 MW in 2007. That number represents growth of 62 percent over the previous year (2006).

As you might suspect, where incentives are the greatest, so too is the growth. Germany is the leading PV market with 1,328 MW in 2007, and represents nearly half (47 percent) of the world PV market. Spain was second in the PV market, with 640 MW. Spain's growth in the PV market in 2007 represents a 480 percent gain over 2006. The United States increased by 57 percent to 220 MW, trailing closely behind Japan at 230 MW. In terms of world solar cell production, Solarbuzz data shows that in 2007 the total number was 3,436 MW. That's up from 2,204 MW in 2006.

These growth numbers, while certainly large, represent only a small dollop of sunshine needed to meet the demand for solar

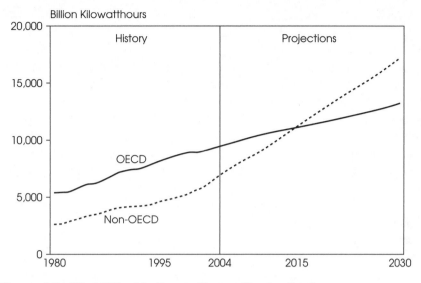

Figure 4.1 World Electric Power Generation by Region

Sources: Figure 61 from EIA, *International Energy Outlook 2007* (Washington, D.C.: U.S. Department of Energy, May 2007), p. 61.

power generation worldwide in the coming years. According to the Energy Information Administration (EIA), world electric power generation is set to soar by 2030 (see Figure 4.1).

Even if only a small sliver of that total projected worldwide demand is met by solar power, we are looking at substantial growth in the demand for solar power worldwide. And, if the growth rate we saw in 2007 is any indication of the growth potential for solar going forward, believe me, solar will be *the* place to be in 2008 and well beyond.

Now I've always been an advocate of following the money when it comes to figuring out what sector represents the next big secular growth wave. How much money is following the solar sector? According to Greentech Media (www.greentechmedia.com), venture capital investment in solar power just in Q1, 2008, was more than $280 million (2008). That's just in one quarter, mind you. In 2007 total venture capital investments in the solar industry was more than $1 billion. This kind of big investment in solar has made it an estimated $18 billion industry as of 2008.

Of course, solar isn't the only area of green energy receiving the big bucks. According to the United Nations' annual *Global Trends in Sustainable Energy Investment 2008* report, global investment capital flows into renewable energy companies reached $100 billion for the first time in ever. More than $30 billion of the total was the result of mergers and acquisitions led by investment banks such as JPMorgan (NYSE: JPM) and Goldman Sachs (NYSE: GS). Indeed, these are the big boys of the financial world, and the UN report truly speaks to the mainstreaming of green technologies and green investments.

In terms of solar's future in the United States, the word "ambitious" once again comes to my mind first. According to the Solar America Initiative (SAI), by 2015 the goal is for solar to provide 5 to 10 gigawatts of electrical generation. By 2030 the SAI wants solar to supply 70 to 100 gigawatts of generating capacity. That's somewhere between 10 and 15 million U.S. households. And the ambitions of the SAI don't stop there. The SAI's goal is for solar to provide 40 percent of all new electrical generation capacity by 2030. If that enormous level were to be achieved, the solar market would be worth somewhere around $30 billion by 2030 (SAI, 2007).

Storing Sunlight in a Bottle

We may not be able to capture lightning in a bottle, but capturing sunlight in a bottle may soon be a reality thanks to researchers at the Massachusetts Institute of Technology. Daniel Nocera, a professor of chemistry and energy at MIT, and postdoctoral fellow Matthew Kanan have figured out how to split water into hydrogen and oxygen cheaply and efficiently at room temperature. The process can later be reversed, allowing the recombination of hydrogen and oxygen in a fuel cell to create carbon-free electricity.

This new process, described in an academic paper, "In Situ Formation of an Oxygen-Evolving Catalyst in Neutral Water Containing Phosphate and Co_{2+}," published in the online edition of *Science* magazine (www.sciencemag.org), effectively details the way solar power could be efficiently stored.

I think this new discovery could have tremendous implications for the future of solar, as it could potentially allow solar power to become a mainstream energy source. Because one of the main issues related to solar power has to do with efficiently storing the collected energy once the sun sets, the Holy Grail, technologically speaking, would be the ability to store the energy and have it at our disposal whenever we need it.

Current solar energy storage processes are both expensive and inefficient; but if the new MIT research can lead to a cheaper and more efficient solar storage method, we might be staring at the turning point toward mass adoption of solar power.

The ChangeWave Thesis

Our proprietary research arm, the ChangeWave Alliance, recently declared 2008 the "Year of Solar" based on a Q1 survey of tech-savvy energy industry professionals. What we found was solar is indeed the wave of the future. We also found that solar is certainly living up to the predictions that it will be the first really big mover in the alternative energy sector.

The report pointed to solar as the alternative energy industry with the most momentum for 2008, and into the next several years. The survey found a shift by corporations toward solar energy as the way to green their energy consumption. Interestingly, this shift is being driven by a relatively new financing technique that allows solar companies to separate the capital expense of the systems they sell and the tax benefits that accrue to the buyer, from the final costs of the electricity produced.

Solar installations, which once consisted mainly of small projects paid for by homeowners or small businesses, are increasingly being financed by companies that offer cheaper electricity or lease payments in exchange for the use of a roof. The solar panels are installed on the roof of an office building or retail outlet, but belong to and are maintained by someone else.

By using this creative approach to financing, a company considering solar power doesn't have to worry about installation costs or changing of the political winds that could result in a reduction of tax incentives. The only thing that matters is the energy cost—which, typically, is 10 percent below market rates.

This new dominant model is called a *power purchase agreement* (PPA), and many solar companies have been using it very effectively to grow their businesses. The key is that PPAs are an attractive vehicle for debt and equity investors, including the likes of Goldman Sachs, Morgan Stanley (NYSE: MS), and GE Energy Financial Services.

The attraction for these top-tier investors is the stable, predictable rate of return. For big retailers and other customers, the price predictability is far more important than having to actively manage their energy budgets according to potential wild fluctuations in the price of energy.

Of paramount concern to individual investors is that the new financing mechanism is creating a surge in demand for solar PV installations.

California Dreaming: Utilities Take a Shine to Solar

Southern California Edison (NYSE: EIX), one of California's "Big 3" utilities, plans to install 50 MW of solar energy per year for five years on commercial rooftops for a 250-MW total commitment. This represents enough electricity to generate power for 162,000 homes.

While California has always paved the way for solar in the United States, this commitment is larger and more concrete than previous projects. In fact, the 250 MW is more than the United States' entire production of solar cells in 2006, and will generate as much electricity as a small coal-fired power plant—with no greenhouse gas emissions.

Among the solar players we track in my *ChangeWave Investing* advisory service, SunPower (Nasdaq: SPWR) is in the best position to gain from this news. The California-based company has set up an extensive dealer network in the state and has its own installations services arm, formerly known as PowerLight, which concentrates on commercial installations.

When you think about all of the untapped rooftops basking in the sun every day in California, and much of the rest of this country, it's easy to dream about the day when a million buildings—commercial and residential—will be covered with solar panels generating clean power from an unlimited green fuel source.

In this case, Edison will lease 65 million square feet of warehouse rooftop space from building owners. The target area is the fast-growing "Inland Empire" of Riverside and San Bernardino counties. The utility will contract for the installation of the arrays and will retain ownership of the solar systems.

The project, once approved, will be financed by a hike in utility rates. The beauty of all of this is that the solar energy will be generated right where it's needed, and Edison is taking advantage of unused rooftop real estate. The alternative approach is to secure a big plot of land in a remote area and then build transmission lines to carry the power to areas of rising demand.

The impact of Edison's commitment will not only affect SunPower, it will also radiate out to companies like China-based Suntech Power Holdings (NYSE: STP) and to other major California utilities such as PG&E Corp. (NYSE: PCG) and San Diego Gas & Electric (NYSE: SRE).

By raising the solar stakes, Edison's move will undoubtedly spur demand in other states, too, which, in turn, will lead to sharp increases in the production of solar cells and all of the materials that are required to make and install them.

As you can see, all of the news and all of the developments in solar, including the data from our Alliance research, points to an acceleration of solar as an integral part of the green technology wave that's fast becoming a driving force for the global economy.

Now with the circumstances in place, what we are seeing right now is a "perfect storm" for both small and large companies that strategically position themselves in the right niches.

At ChangeWave, we've studied the top solar companies around the world to help find the best of the best. Many of these firms manufacture solar PV cells, and others occupy the supply link in the solar value chain by providing the feedstock (polysilicon) and silicon wafers that form the substrate for the vast majority of solar cells today. Now let's take a look at some of the brightest stars in the solar space.

A Concentrated Effort

The solar sector is replete with new technologies, and one of the most promising is concentrated photovoltaic, or CPV. As the name suggests, CPV is all about doing more with less.

Traditional photovoltaic panels, such as the kind we've discussed in this chapter, produce electricity based on variables like the quality of the silicon used in the cells, the size of the solar cell, and the amount of sun exposure and the efficiency of its conversion technology. Concentrated photovoltaics take a different approach.

Remember when you were a kid and you would use a magnifying glass to focus the sun's rays on one area and how much hotter that spot became? Well, scientists have applied that idea to solar energy to dramatically increase the amount of energy generated by the sun.

(Continues)

(*Continued*)

When you insert a more-efficient solar cell in the path of all that energy, you become much, much more efficient in producing solar power. One company making this possible is Emcore (Nasdaq: EMKR). Their Generation 2 CPV array combines light-magnifying reflectors with highly efficient, smaller solar cells. This combination allows Emcore's solar cells to realize greater power production at a lower cost-per-watt than other solar producers.

The goal in the industry is to make solar as inexpensive as possible, and to generate power at a cost per kilowatt-hour that is on par with fossil fuel-derived electricity. Emcore's high-efficiency cells could hold the key toward achieving this goal of cost parity.

Emcore is the kind of company creating the innovations at the bleeding edge of the green revolution. But Emcore is not alone. As of the summer of 2008, I know of at least a dozen startups working on ways to use mirrors and lenses to concentrate sunlight hundreds of times onto tiny, highly efficient solar cells. Even if just a few of these companies are successful, it will mean greater and greater opportunity to invest in the CPV space. As the old saying goes, the future is certainly looking bright for solar.

Solar Superstars

The following companies are some of my favorite ways to play the solar wave. Now remember, when it comes to investing rapid change is always an operative factor. But the overriding solar sector drivers we've outlined here in this chapter should mean much more growth ahead for the following solar superstars.

Ascent Solar

Silicon-based photovoltaics are good and they will be here for a long time. And while silicon accounts for more than 90 percent of all solar cells manufactured today, thin-film photovoltaics are rapidly moving out of the lab and into commercial production.

With Ascent Solar (Nasdaq: ASTI), you have an opportunity to invest in the next big wave hitting the solar industry—thin-film technology for solar cells, a market that's growing at an excess of 70 percent annually.

Keep these interesting factoids in mind: In one minute, the sun provides enough energy to supply the world's energy needs for one year. In one day, it provides more energy than the world's population could consume in 27 years. The sun's energy is free, and the supply is abundant. All we need to do is find a way to capture it.

Integrating flexible thin-film solar cells (as opposed to hard cells) into *building-integrated PVs* (BIPVs) and consumer electronics–integrated PVs (EIPVs) is coming to our world fast—and this wave has just started.

Imagine a building whose internal structure creates enough electrical power to run its lights and air conditioning. Imagine a home generating enough electricity from its roof and windows to sell back to the power company on sunny days. Imagine military field equipment with the technology built inside to recharge batteries and supply enough electrical power to run off the battery on sunny days.

Ascent Solar has developed the technology and know-how to make BIPV and EIPV a reality beginning as early as 2008. At ChangeWave, we tracked ASTI prior to its IPO, but we really took notice when Norway's Fortune 500 member, Norsk Hydro, made a $9.2-million investment in this tiny company, buying a 23 percent stake in ASTI.

In 2006, Ascent had spun out from ITN Energy Systems, a research-and-development company that works on government and private technology development, largely for the aerospace and defense industries. (Today, ITN still provides at cost, a variety of administrative services such as facilities management, equipment maintenance, human resources, procurement, information technology services and accounting).

Norsk is a very big building materials supplier in Europe and it took almost two years to review every private and public thin-film (i.e., nonsilicon-based) PV technology worldwide. Its conclusion? ASTI's technology was head and shoulders ahead of the rest of the world, and it bought 23 percent of the company (with rights to raise its stake to 35 percent by buying another 1.5 million shares) because it saw such a bright future for BIPV and EIPV solar applications.

Here is what Norsk knows and what key ChangeWave Alliance members in the industry are saying as well:

1. Building-integrated is one of the fastest-growing segments of the PV industry. When PV panels are integrated into a building during construction, the incremental costs of the system are reduced while the building owner is provided with tangible, cost-saving advantages such as significantly reduced demand

for peak electricity, reduced transmission losses and a backup power source.

2. BIPV best demonstrates the multifunctionality of PV. BIPV gives buildings the opportunity to become more self-sufficient by allowing them to generate their own electricity rather than merely consume energy. PV integrated into a building can, as a second function, provide shade and insulation and help to control the interior climate.

3. Thin-film PV modules are more suitable for BIPV. Crystalline silicon modules not only lack the aesthetic and physical properties required for BIPV installations, but their significantly higher cost per area makes them uneconomical for project managers.

4. In the developing world, BIPV installations are the most desirable. This is because BIPV doesn't use any extra space and because the material savings from replacing ordinary construction material with BIPV substantially reduces the cost of the installed PV system, and thus the cost of PV electricity.

Though a development stage company, Ascent appears to be the first firm out of the gate to manufacture large, roll format, PV modules in commercial quantities that use a highly efficient thin-film copper-indium-gallium-diselenide (CIGS) absorbing layer on a flexible high-temperature plastic substrate.

Ascent has produced and tested small-scale demonstration samples of their CIGS PV products at the laboratory level and for the Norsk people, but it has not yet produced any products in commercial quantities. The company is dedicating most of the $14 million it netted from its July 2006 IPO and the subsequent $10 million from Norsk to establish a 1.5 MW pilot-scale production line.

Clearly, Norsk is convinced that the ASTI production facility works. The production line is expected to begin operations in Q1 2008. Successful performance of the pilot production line should prove out the manufacturing processes, products and market acceptance to enable a transition into large, full-scale commercial manufacturing of BIPV and EIPV CIGS products.

Energy Conversion Devices

Energy Conversion Devices (Nasdaq: ENER; ECD Ovonics), which you learned about in the previous chapter, invents, engineers, and develops new materials and products in the fields of alternative energy technology and information technology. The company's products include nickel-metal hydride (NiMH) via their joint venture Cobasys with ChevronTexaco (see Chapter 3). But there is much more to ECD Ovonics than just batteries. It also owns the leader in photovoltaic roofing.

Using its proprietary thin-film a-Si alloy materials, ECD Ovonics has developed the most cost-effective solar cell on the market. Not only do their solar cells absorb light more efficiently than crystalline counterparts, but their thickness can be 100 times less, thereby significantly reducing materials cost.

ECD Ovonics holds the current world records for both large- and small-area conversion efficiency for a-Si solar cells, as measured by the DOE's National Renewable Energy Laboratory. This is an exploding technology in the more energy-efficient green world, especially in Europe, where the EU-member states now have regulations requiring PV-membrane roofing in many areas.

There is no doubt that the very smart folks at ECD Ovonics have taken their time to get where they are today. Having gone public in the mid-1980s, it's taken over 20 years to get to the point where the company's ideas have caught up with industry demand. But all the regulatory and energy stars are now in alignment, and there is simply no better "double play," that is to say, both hybrid batteries and solar PV, than ECD Ovonics.

LDK Solar

China-based LDK Solar (Nasdaq: LDK) has been producing silicon wafers for solar-cell manufacturers since 2005, and it produces both the polysilicon ingots and the wafers used in PV manufacturing. LDK has many positive factors working for it, not the least of which is its strong position in the PV food chain and solid profit margins. The longer-term picture for LDK will be very bright.

LDK sells to the major Chinese PV manufacturer Suntech Power (Nasdaq: STP), as well as other Chinese solar companies. Based on the robust outlook for demand, LDK has a huge new plant coming on line in 2009 that's expected to double output.

SunPower Corporation

SunPower (Nasdaq: SPWR) is a leading player in photovoltaic manufacturing sector, providing systems for homes and businesses. SunPower's high-efficiency solar cells and solar panels generate up to 50 percent more power than conventional solar technologies and offer attractive packaging that doesn't scream "solar."

In January 2008 the company announced the completion of a 390-kilowatt solar power system at the Sam's Club in Chino, California. The store is the first of seven Wal-Mart (NYSE: WMT) facilities in California install to SunPower solar systems, totaling 4.6 megawatts, and is part of a major purchase for approximately 22 Wal-Mart stores, Sam's Clubs, and distribution centers in Hawaii and California. The stores included in this pilot project are expected to achieve savings over their current utility rates beginning on the first day of operation.

In areas where Wal-Mart leads, others are sure to follow. This is especially true when it comes to improving the corporate bottom line. Another way to get exposure to SunPower is through technology firm Cypress Semiconductor (Nasdaq: CY), which owns 65 percent of the company.

Suntech Power Holdings

China-based Suntech Power Holdings (Nasdaq: STP) is one of the largest solar energy companies in the world based on production output and capacity of solar cells and modules. STP has developed an advanced process to manufacture PV cells cost-effectively at a large production scale with high conversion efficiencies (i.e., how much sun energy is converted to electrical power). Studies show that STP's average conversion efficiency rates of its monocrystalline and multicrystalline silicon PV cells reached 16.5 percent and 15 percent, respectively, versus average ranges of 12 percent to 17 percent and 11 percent to 16 percent.

In Q1 2008, STP announced it is taking a minority interest in Nitol Solar, an independent polysilicon producer, for up to $100 million. This relationship is not new. STP entered into a multiyear supply agreement with Nitol in August 2007 for the supply of polysilicon to STP from 2009 to 2015, and such deals diminish STP's exposure to spot-market purchases, improving visibility and potentially raising gross margins. Suntech great fundamentals—particularly its scale of production and industry leadership—will likely keep the shares shining well into the future.

Yingli Green Energy

Based in China, Yingli Green Energy (Nasdaq: YGE) sells polysilicon ingots and wafers, photovoltaic cells and modules, and integrated photovoltaic systems. The company has secured all of its polysilicon needs for 2008 and most of its needs for 2009. This is critical because the world's polysilicon supply will ramp to an oversupply by mid-2009.This will lower the cost of solar cells as much as 50 percent.

That drop in cost greatly benefits Yingli and will trigger further demand in utilities and other large solar users. As we've discussed already, the cost of solar is rapidly heading toward the Holy Grail of grid parity (where the total cost of solar is on par with fossil fuel energy). As this occurs, it doesn't take a genius to figure out what happens to the solar industry.

Yingli's vertically integrated business model enables it to capture profit at nearly every stage of the PV industry value chain and with-stand, or capitalize on, the fluctuating profit margins of products at these different stages. The company plans to gradually expand annual production capacity of polysilicon ingots and wafers, PV cells and PV modules to 400 MW by the end of 2008, and to 600 MW by the end of 2009. This will position Yingli as one of the lowest-cost producers in the industry.

Any way you slice it (bad pun for the way solar wafers are cut), YGE looks very attractive. It has a compelling valuation versus its competitors, one of the lowest cost structures, a secure near-term supply of polysilicon, and a high-quality reputation.

Value Chain Stock Recap

- Raw Silicon Manufacturers: LDK Solar (LDK), Yingli Green Energy (Nasdaq: YGE)
- Silicon Wafer/Ingot Manufacturer: LDK Solar, Yingli Green Energy
- Highest-Efficiency Solar-Cell Maker: SunPower (Nasdaq: SPWR)
- Lowest-Cost Solar-Cell Maker: Suntech Power Holdings (Nasdaq: STP), Yingli Green Energy
- Next-Generation Thin-Film Solar Cells (Non-Silicon): Ascent Solar (Nasdaq: ASTI), Energy Conversion Devices (Nasdaq: ENER)

A Solar Epilogue

As you've just seen, the future for solar is very bright indeed. I think solar could be the next really big money-making opportunity for investors who want to be green and make green.

But sunshine isn't the only source of green out there. Along with the sun, an essential element to a greener, better world is clean water. And while you might take for granted the cleanliness and availability of water, the rest of the world—including the United States—has some big challenges with regards to water.

What are those challenges and how can investor's profit from solving the need for a cleaner, greener water supply? That's what you'll find out in Chapter 5.

Surveys Say: Solar Strong, Gaining Corporate Ground

In the ChangeWave Alliance's December 2007 survey comparing emerging power sources, solar rates well ahead of wind, biomass and all other alternative energy technologies. What's more, solar enjoyed the most momentum going forward.

Solar led in each of the following areas:

- **Most Rapid Economic Growth—Past 12 Months:** When asked which alternative energy sector has experienced the fastest growth during the past year, solar (49 percent) topped the list—up a whopping 14 points since a February 2007 survey.
- **Most Rapid Economic Growth—Next 12 to 24 Months:** Going forward, respondent saw solar as experiencing the most rapid growth in the industry for the next one to two years, up 20 points to 38 percent.
- **Most Momentum—Next Five Years:** Over the long term, solar also retains its strength, as 31 percent of respondents (a 5-point increase) said it will be the top sector for the next five years.

Figure 4.2 illustrates solar's dominance among ChangeWave Alliance survey respondents.

In March 2008 the ChangeWave Alliance completed its first survey on the energy-efficiency practices of corporations, and once again we see the vast promise of solar underscored.

Among the companies that currently use local power generation, one-half have solar systems installed—more than twice the second place alternative energy technology.

More importantly, when asked about which type of alternative energy equipment they planned to install, solar jumped to nearly three quarters, better than triple the rate of the second-place choice.

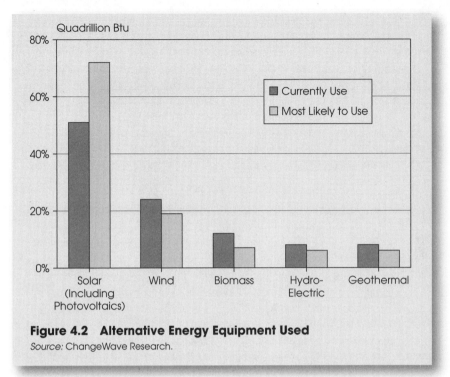

Figure 4.2 Alternative Energy Equipment Used
Source: ChangeWave Research.

What's This ChangeWave Alliance All About?

When it comes to picking the best stocks in the fastest-moving sectors of the market, we pride ourselves on staying months ahead of the conventional thinking on Wall Street.

This is possible thanks to the ChangeWave Alliance, our network of more than 15,000 experts that we constantly survey in order to uncover the next big green (and other) trends, and to identify new breakout companies.

Our Alliance members are IT purchasing managers, software engineers, telecom buyers, doctors, scientists, and industry experts. All are focused on the same mission: helping you profit from change.

It seems like whenever I bring up the Alliance, I inevitably get a few questions that essentially ask me the same things: What is the Alliance, and why does it matter to me?

First, the ChangeWave Alliance is, in essence, a co-op of credentialed, profiled *ChangeWave Investing* field experts who spend their

(Continues)

(Continued)

everyday professional lives working on the front lines of technology and related industries and professions. As in the open-source software world, Alliance members, in return for free access to the end results research of the community, contribute their eyes, ears, and brains to our investment intelligence–gathering community.

Our goal for the ChangeWave Alliance is to improve the traditional investment research model by removing the conflicts and roadblocks to gathering and distributing unbiased buy/sell/hold investment advice. In short, we have changed the model of investment research into a team sport.

The ChangeWave Alliance can significantly improve the odds of picking winning stocks. Here's the math behind this bold claim.

More than a decade ago, a brilliant young technologist named Bob Metcalfe was trying to sell a new networking technology called *Ethernet.* He coined the term "Metcalfe's Law" to suggest the unique logic behind the power of a network. Kevin Kelly describes this math in his seminal work, *New Rules for the New Economy,* "Mathematics holds that the sum value of a network increases as a square of the number of its members. In other words, as the number of nodes (connections) in a network increases arithmetically, the value of the network increases exponentially."

The Internet itself is perhaps the best example of this "network effect." E-mail wasn't valuable to you until a critical mass of people you communicate with had it and started to use it on a regular basis. In short, in a network, the more plentiful things become, the more valuable they become. When you add to this calculus the many academic studies that find that the more diverse a group is, the higher the quality of decision making, you start to get the logic behind the power of the ChangeWave Alliance.

When someone applies and is accepted into the ChangeWave Alliance network (only about one in three applications are accepted), the network becomes more valuable to the existing participants. The next invitee who joins makes the network more valuable to you, and so on and so on. Every new member increases the richness and reach of the entire network's intelligence gathering and processing. Each new node in the ChangeWave Alliance network raises the odds of the success for all members of the Alliance.

Every time we increase the richness and reach of our intelligence, we add another 100 or so investment intelligence–gathering and analysis research hours to our system. And every quality research hour we add to the system means we get closer to finding our next Change-Wave sweet spot and, we hope, a few more monster stocks.

What makes this network work in the context of discovering and communicating investment intelligence is its common focus, protocol, language, and peer-review improvement process. Whereas other network investment communities have a group of many but the power of none, we have the power of many and the focus of one.

Rather than being the tower of investment babble, or essentially an entertainment media, our ChangeWave Alliance members actually help identify fundamental waves of change, and they help us identify the companies best positioned to profit from that change.

I am proud to say that the ChangeWave Alliance has now grown to more than 15,000 members strong as of Q1 2008. This growth is far beyond anything I imagined even a few short years ago. And we're still making gains in new people and new professionals who bring their unique perspectives to our table.

CHAPTER

Water, Water, Everywhere, Nor Any Drop to Drink

SYMPATHIZING WITH THE ANCIENT MARINER

Water, water, everywhere,
And all the boards did shrink;
Water, water, everywhere,
Nor any drop to drink.
    —Samuel Coleridge, "The Rime of the Ancient Mariner"

The lament of the mariner in Coleridge's classic poem is an apt metaphor for the world's water situation in the twenty-first century. Water, at least in the aggregate, is not in short supply. One look at any satellite photo of the earth from space shows that we are basically one big blue marble dotted with a smidge of green, tan, and brown.

The globe is teeming with H_2O. Nearly three quarters of the earth's surface is covered with water. Unfortunately, only a very tiny percentage of that water is clean, potable, and fit for human and animal consumption. Much like energy, the problem with water isn't its availability. The world has ample supplies of energy and water, but what the world lacks is cheap, clean energy. The world also lacks cheap, clean water.

69

The earth's total water supply is estimated to be 330 million cubic miles, and each cubic mile contains more than one trillion gallons. The problem is that 96 percent of that water is found in the oceans and is saline. Another 7 million cubic miles is tied up in ice-caps and glaciers, and another 3 million or so cubic miles is in the earth's atmosphere.

Freshwater sources, such as ground water, freshwater lakes, and rivers represent about 2 million cubic miles of fresh water. If you do the math, you'll see that it comes out to approximately 99.7 percent of all the water on earth that is virtually unavailable for human consumption. Unfortunately, much of that remaining 0.3 percent is inaccessible due to unreachable locations and depths well below the earth's surface.

As they say in real estate, the three biggest factors are location, location, location. And while the variables might not be as simple for water, location is a huge factor in the overall water equation. Because large freshwater supplies are not distributed uniformly over the earth, water has always been one of the most precious—and fought over—commodities. In fact, tales of the political intrigue throughout history aimed at controlling water resources could fill volumes. For our purposes, it's sufficient to say that water has been a source of geopolitical tensions for virtually as long as societies have existed, and I fully expect water and water issues to continue affecting the globe well into the twenty-first century and beyond.

One recent example of societal conflict over water is worth mentioning because it connects to my earlier thesis on energy security. In the generally arid Middle East, water is a source (one of many) of conflict between Israel and its Arab neighbors. Water is also a big subject of contention between Egypt and Sudan, Turkey, Syria, and Iraq. In fact, the march toward the 1967 Six-Day War was spurred on by the water dispute between Israel and Syria over control over the Jordan River.

A lack of water in the Middle East adds to the conflicting tribal and religious differences in the region, and all of this adds to the overall instability of a region that supplies the world with oil. My point is that water scarcity is an issue that needs to be dealt with worldwide because if we can get cleaner water to more people—especially in the Middle East—we can help ameliorate the world's tensions.

Of course, the best solution for improving the energy security problem is to wean ourselves completely off of oil and to remove the need for using a commodity primary found below the surface of countries whose borders are likely to be in a state of conflict for many more decades. One of the goals of this book is to show you the companies that are helping the world do just that.

You're Going to Drive Me to Drinking

The world is thirsty, and it's getting thirstier by the day. As the tremendous economic growth of developing nations such as China and India ramps up, and as world population growth continues to surge over the next decade and well beyond, the world is going to need a lot more watering holes.

This increasing thirst by a more populous, more urban/industrialized world, has already taken place over the past five decades. By some estimates, global demand for water has more than tripled over the past half century. And where is that demand for water being used? Well, much of it is used in agriculture. In fact, worldwide agriculture drinks up about three quarters of the world's freshwater. In the United States agriculture accounts for roughly 40 percent of freshwater use; however, another 40 percent goes to industrial purposes such as cooling thermal power plants. As the world grows, it's going to need more food, more fresh drinking water, and more water for industrial purposes. Are you seeing a pattern here? Water and energy demand—along with the need for innovative solutions—are on parallel growth paths. And much like energy, the future of water is riddled with challenges.

One of those challenges is water withdrawal. At the turn of the twenty-first century global *water withdrawal* (the removal of freshwater from resources and/or reservoirs for use in agriculture, industry, and drinking) was estimated to be about 1,000 cubic miles ($4,000 \text{ km}^3$), or approximately 30 percent of the world's total accessible freshwater supply. By 2025 global water withdrawal may reach 70 percent. Why? Well, because our thirsty world has already overpumped ground water to the point where we've exceeded natural replenishment by more than 160 km^3, or about 4 percent of total withdrawals. As more water is usurped by a thirsty populace each year, it's easy to see why we could be facing a serious water shortage problem over the next two decades.

Here is why this situation is so serious. According to the World Health Organization, over 1 billion people currently lack access to clean water supplies. Over 2 million people are thought to perish each year because of unsafe drinking water and poor sanitary conditions. Waterborne diseases account for roughly 80 percent of infections in the developing world, including nearly 4 billion cases of diarrhea each year. Approximately 200 million people are infected with the parasitic diseases, and intestinal worms infect about 10 percent of the developing world's population. Finally, about 3,900 children die each day from waterborne diseases (Wallerstein, 2006). As you can see, clean water is a serious problem around the globe, and just think what will happen if the situation continues worsening. This is a global problem that begs for a solution from companies with new, innovative, and greener ideas.

Now, if you think that water is an issue confined only to the developing world, think again. The sustainable withdrawal of freshwater also is an issue in the United States. Rapid demand increase for clean water has already created shortage situations in parts of the country, and shortages in one area of the country are likely to make other areas susceptible to shortages in the future.

There is another reason why water may be at issue in the United States, and that reason holds true for much of the rest of the globe. You see, to bring clean water to the masses you need a serious infrastructure. Major cities in the United States and abroad are operating on infrastructure—water pipes, power grids, transport systems—that are aging and badly in need of upgrades or replacement. Trillions (yes, with a T) of dollars will be spent during the next decade to repair this infrastructure and bring it up to standards for the twenty-first century.

If You Build It, They Will Drink

I've seen some estimates that say over $40 trillion will be needed to modernize urban water, electricity, and transportation systems globally by 2030. In the United States, it will likely cost nearly $2 trillion to upgrade our current water and energy infrastructures. Of course, it's hard to say with precision what kind of money will need to be spent just to get the water portion of that infrastructure up to where it should be, but it's safe to assume that a lot of capital is going to be devoted to this cause.

One U.S. government agency did make a prediction about how much it would cost the country to upgrade its aging water infrastructure. In a May 2008 report, the Environmental Protection Agency (EPA) stated the United States needs to invest $202.5 billion in its wastewater infrastructure due to aging facilities, rising water quality standards and population growth. That dollar amount is nearly 9 percent more than the capital investment the federal agency said was needed in 2000. According to the EPA's report to Congress, $134.4 billion will be required to upgrade waste treatment systems, $54.8 billion for sewer overflows, and $9 billion for storm water management.

This focus on repair and replacement of the water infrastructure in the United States, and the massive build-out required to support the growth in emerging markets and the developing world, are the two big areas of opportunity for investors who want to benefit from the world's growing thirst.

Want more evidence of a failing U.S. water infrastructure? How about the report card from the nation's leading organization of engineers? In 2005 the American Society of Civil Engineers, released a report that gave the nation's drinking water infrastructure a grade of D–. The nation's dams fared only slightly better, receiving a D+ grade from the engineering group. As you can see, the U.S. water infrastructure is not exactly a model student. In fact, it seems to me that it needs a private tutor.

The needs of the U.S. water infrastructure, while certainly large, pale in comparison to China, which is undergoing the biggest infrastructure boom in history. A quarter century of rapid urbanization and industrialization has basically overwhelmed that nation's water infrastructure. According to the Chinese government's current Five-Year Plan, which runs through 2010, $30 billion will be needed to fix the nation's urban water supply, and $40 billion will be required to modernize wastewater treatment.

A Tall Drink of Green Water

What are the solutions to the world's water situation? Upgrading water pipes, sewage plants, dams, and reservoirs will no doubt be part of the solution. What's also likely to be part of the solution—and what's more in step with the ideas in this book—is a growing number of cleaner, greener, water solutions.

Greener water solutions consist of employing high-tech methods and devices to water purification systems. Desalination and the use of nano-based membranes are the next wave of green water solutions.

Desalinization is the conversion of seawater into freshwater fit for drinking, agricultural, and industrial use. Desalination is a costly proposition, and so it's no surprise that countries with a lot of available capital are the ones with the biggest desalinization plants currently operating. Cash-rich and freshwater-poor Saudi Arabia is the biggest user of desalinized seawater. The country accounts for about one quarter of all desalinized seawater worldwide.

One reason why desalinization is a costly proposition has to do with the tremendous amount of energy needed to fuel the desalinization process. Reducing the energy required in the desalinization process via methods such as reverse osmosis membrane technology will be a key component in the battle to contain costs.

Another promising new technology is nano-based membranes. Filtering water through membranes is not new. Membranes that separate the unwanted elements in water from the water itself have been used for over a decade, but now the level of technological sophistication is becoming greater and more refined. There are now nano-based membranes that are designed to screen out and clean nearly all forms of harmful pollutants. Bacteria, viruses, pesticides, and other unwanted elements can all be filtered out of water supplies, making those supplies safe for human and animal consumption.

The technology currently being developed will likely continue becoming better and better, especially as demand for clean water increases. Much like energy, the demand equation for water will drive entrepreneurs to create solutions to the world's water shortage challenges. And like energy, many of the world's biggest companies are going to jump into the fray. There will also be a few niche market players that solve a particular problem confronting the water industry. But where are these opportunities and what is the current state of the water industry? For answers to these questions, I'm going to turn to the water industry experts of the ChangeWave Alliance.

The Alliance Dips Its Toe into the Water

Amidst mounting concerns about scarcity and the quality of the world's water supply, ChangeWave Research has conducted a series of surveys on water industry trends and opportunities. The most recent survey prior to this book's publication was completed in February 2008.

ChangeWave's survey findings point to increased water project spending for 2008, albeit slightly less than the levels of project spending in recent years, with over two thirds (67 percent) of water industry respondents saying overall spending on water projects will increase over the next 12 months. The survey also asked industry respondents about spending in specific regions of the world. Figure 5.1 shows the percentage of industry respondents who think overall water spending will increase in each region.

Asia (71 percent) ranks as the top geographical region for water spending increases over the next 12 months, followed by North America (65 percent) and the Middle East (64 percent). When asked to name the specific country set to experience the biggest

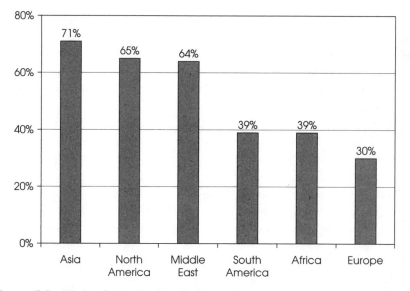

Figure 5.1   Water Spending by Region
Sources: ChangeWave Research

spending increase, 45 percent cited China. Another 13 percent said the United States.

And which specific technologies, products, and/or processes do Alliance members see companies investing the most money in to improve water efficiency? Nearly one in four (23 percent) believe that water conservation and reuse is the area that will see the most investment. In a tie for second place was (1) reverse osmosis, (2) filtration, and (3) membrane technology, each of which garnered a respective 11 percent of respondents who say that segment will see the greatest spending.

In terms of which water industry sectors were likely to benefit most over the next 12 to 24 months, water infrastructure repair and replacement was by far the biggest winner, with 73 percent of respondents citing that sector as the one likely to attract the most public and private spending. Wastewater treatment (46 percent), water filtration (14 percent), and desalinization (14 percent) rounded out the list. When asked which water sectors have the most momentum going forward, wastewater treatment and water infrastructure were once again seen as attracting the most spending over the next two years.

Splashing Around in the Water Investment Pool

We've come to the good part of the water story, where you learn how to splash around in the water investment pool. The caveat I mentioned in Chapter 4 bears repeating at this point and remains in effect throughout this book: When it comes to picking leading companies in leading industries, there's nothing like having your own research team made up of industry experts. And which companies do our industry experts think will lead the way forward in the water space?

It should come as no surprise that infrastructure giant General Electric (NYSE: GE) has the highest profile amongst water industry experts. GE is by far the biggest fish in the pond. The company's Water & Process Technologies division has gone on a buying spree in the past few years, scooping up filtration and purification firms such as ZENON Environmental to gain its membrane technologies.

The problem with General Electric is that as an investor, you cannot just buy shares in their water business. Because GE is such a huge conglomerate, any investment in GE shares comes with a whole bunch of other businesses you either don't want—or that are holding GE's share price down. Until GE spins off divisions such as its Water & Process Technologies, and until it allows the public to trade those shares apart from their other businesses, an investment in GE for the sake of its water business is going to be a far removed proposition.

Siemens (NYSE: SI) is another industrial behemoth making a big splash in the water infrastructure market, but much like GE, water accounts for only a small portion of the company's business. Siemens, too, has been on a buying spree in recent years, acquiring companies such USFilter to help bolster its position in the water purification market. The problem with Siemens for investors is the same one we have with GE. There is no way to just invest in their water business. At best you are going to get just some of the benefit of the company's water operations when you own the stock. And while there might be good reasons to own either GE or SI shares at any given time, the exposure you get from water won't be enough to make or break either company's share price performance. I much prefer taking a more focused route when investing in the water stocks.

Fortunately, there are ways investors can get exposure to specific companies that concentrate primarily on the business of water. One of the companies identified by our Alliance research was environment services firm Veolia Environnement (VE). This company's provides water and wastewater services, including management and operation of drinking water plants, wastewater decontamination and recycling plants, drinking water distribution networks and wastewater collection networks. I think Veolia is the best at what it does, and there presence worldwide is bound to grow as the world builds out its water infrastructure.

Another water industry company I like is Basin Water (Nasdaq: BWTR), which sells water treatment systems (its ion-exchange system removes arsenic, nitrate, perchlorate, uranium, and chromium VI to nondetectable levels) to a range of customers including two of the largest investor-owned water utilities in the United States. I suspect that removing impurities in the water supply is going to become increasingly important to a health-conscious U.S. population concerned with environmental and green issues.

Other notable companies identified by our Alliance as leading players in the water industry were: Water and utility firm American States Water Company (NYSE: AWR); water purification firm Calgon Carbon (NYSE: CCC); water flow equipment maker Flowserve (NYSE: FLS); water pump and fluid control maker Gorman-Rupp Company (AMEX: GRC), and water treatment product firm Nalco (NYSE: NLC).

Why Not Use a Bucket?

Rather than trying to pick the best water stocks, one way to approach an investment in the water industry is to use a "bucket." The bucket in this case is an exchange-traded fund (ETF) that contains many of the best water companies operating today.

The bucket of water stocks I like is the PowerShares Water Resources (AMEX: PHO). This exchange-traded fund resembles a mutual fund in the sense you are getting exposure to many companies in one industry. But, unlike mutual funds, ETFs are traded on an exchange and bought and sold just like regular common stocks. The growth of ETFs over the past several years has been one of Wall Street's biggest stories. And while I am not the biggest fan of ETFs out there, I do think that there are times when investors can use them effectively.

The beauty of the PowerShares Water Resources is that it gives you exposure to each of the companies that were highest rated in our February 2008 water industry survey (comprising approximately one third of the PHO holdings). PHO also has a well-balanced portfolio, with no single stock representing more than 4 percent of the total. If after reading this chapter you're convinced that water stocks belong in your portfolio, then I do suggest taking a look at PHO. Generally speaking, I like to buy individual stocks, but sometimes there's nothing as good as a bucket full of profit opportunity.

Toweling Off—and on to the Power Grid

Now let's dry ourselves off and move from the need to upgrade the water infrastructure, to the need to upgrade our aging power infrastructure. As you'll see in a moment, the need to upgrade the power grid both worldwide and in the United States is on par with the need to build out the water infrastructure.

Many of the same growth drivers are present in both water and power, and as with water, identifying the subsectors and the companies in those subsectors with the greatest profit potential is the trick to making real green. That trick is the subject of Chapter 6.

CHAPTER 6

Avoiding "Grid" Lock
THE POWERS THAT BE ARE GOING SMART

Turn up the lights. I don't want to go home in the dark.

—O. Henry

When I use the term "gridlock," the first thing that should come into your mind is being stuck in traffic. In this chapter, the term gridlock—or rather grid lock—has a little different meaning. When I use the word "grid" here, I am speaking not of our nation's congested freeway system, but rather of another form of mass transit. That form is the mass transit of energy from power generation station to your home or business.

Much like our current water infrastructure, our nation's energy infrastructure was built many decades ago. And like our water systems, our electrical power grid is a fantastic achievement. In fact, I'd have to say that the electrification of America is perhaps the greatest achievement of the entire twentieth century. Just think about how beautiful this achievement is. You come home, you flip the switch, and voila! Your lights are on. Press a few buttons and, boom, there's your TV, computer, stereo, electric stovetop, coffee maker, blender, and so on. Oh, and don't forget about the power keeping your food fresh round the clock in your refrigerator.

Indeed, I am a big fan of the electric grid, because it makes living in the modern world as we know it possible. But, despite all of its virtues, the power grid is not without its problems. The grid itself—power generation stations, power lines, transformers, circuit breakers, on-site electric metering devices, and so on—is starting to show signs of age. Already, the grid is susceptible to widespread blackouts and brownouts that cost our nation billions of dollars in lost productivity.

Another big drawback of the current grid is inefficiency. It's estimated that the North American power grid bleeds off about 20 percent of the energy it generates as it moves through transmission lines. This degradation in energy quantity also leads to a decrease in the quality of energy needed to run a twenty-first-century continent. But perhaps the biggest drawback of the current grid system is its lack of information.

The grid, for all its virtues, isn't very smart. The grid transmits electrons from power generation station to end user without any real feedback. This model works most of the time, but it doesn't work very efficiently, nor does it allow for a sophisticated and specialized use of our current resources. So, what must be done to modernize the grid and get us into the twenty-first century? What will be required to avoid grid lock? More importantly, how can you, the individual investor, make money from this need to modernize the power grid? Let's find out.

A Vision for the Modern Grid

I am not a super big fan of government reports. Every once in a while, however, there's a report by a government agency that really hits the mark. One such report is *A Vision for the Modern Grid* by the National Energy Technology Laboratory (NETL), a division of the U.S. Department of Energy. As the title suggests, this report laid out some great suggestions on what's needed to transform our current grid into the grid needed to meet the tremendous power demands not only of the present, but of a society with an ever voracious appetite for power that's likely to grow exponentially over the next several decades.

The modern grid vision put forth by the NETL focused on six primary goals. The first goal was to make the grid more reliable. A reliable grid provides dependable power whenever and wherever it is needed. And while the dependability factor in the current grid is truly amazing, if—or inevitably when—there is a problem the current grid isn't well equipped to identify it. The new modern grid must provide ample warning of any mounting problems, and it must withstand those unforeseen yet inevitable disturbances without breaking down. The modern grid needs to, in effect, take corrective action *before* most users are affected.

The second goal for the new grid is that it must be more secure. A secure grid should be able to weather both physical and cyber attacks without suffering any large-scale blackouts. It also must be less susceptible to natural disasters like hurricanes, tornadoes, heat waves, and earthquakes.

The third element cited by the NETL to bring the grid into the twenty-first century is that it must become more economic. An economic grid must operate in accordance with the basic laws of supply and demand. With greater reliance on a traditional supply/demand model, the report argues that the result will be fair prices and adequate electricity supplies. Now this is a very interesting thing to find in a government report. The realization that, in essence, the electricity market must become more like the rest of the free market is a truly exciting and opportunity-generating development.

The fourth goal of the modern grid is that it must become more efficient. We've already seen how the grid bleeds excess electricity, but that's not the only aspect of improved efficiency required. The NETL report argues, quite correctly in my view, that an efficient grid takes advantage of investments that lead to cost control, reduced transmission and distribution electrical losses, more efficient power production, and improved asset utilization. New methods to control the flow of power to reduce transmission congestion and allow access to low-cost generating sources—including renewable energy generation sources—must be made available.

The next goal of the modern grid is that it needs to become more environmentally friendly; that is to say, it needs to become greener. An environmentally friendly grid reduces its overall environmental impact in multiple ways, including new power generation methods, new transmission methods, better distribution, improved storage, and reduced consumption.

The final of these six goals of a modern grid is safety. The new grid must be safer. It must do no harm to the public or to grid workers, and it must be sensitive to users who depend on it as a medical necessity.

Now these goals, while indeed noble, are not the easiest to achieve. When it comes to the power grid, we've got quite a hefty infrastructure to contend with. Having said this, there are technologies being developed by a number of excellent publicly traded companies doing their part to modernize the grid. I'll have much more to say on this topic in a moment.

Seven Valuable Virtues of the Modern Grid

Everyone has heard of the seven deadly sins. And if you're anything like me, you've been guilty of committing more than one on numerous occasions. Now when it comes to the modern grid, we can use the seven deadly sins model and turn it on its head. The modern grid will have what I call the seven valuable virtues.

These virtues were identified by the NETL in their aforementioned report on how best to modernize the existing power grid. Let's take a look at each before we connect the dots on how to make a pile of green off the coming grid modernization.

The first valuable virtue of the modern grid is that it will possess the ability to heal itself. The modernized grid will be equipped with technology that lets it perform continuous self-assessments. These self-assessments will help the grid detect, analyze, and respond to problems quickly. This self-healing concept for the modern grid will infuse it with what the NETL describes as its own "immune system," or what is, in effect, the ability to maintain grid reliability, security, affordability, power quality, and efficiency.

The self-healing grid will employ modern technologies that can acquire data, execute decision-support algorithms, avert or limit interruptions, dynamically control the flow of power, and restore power service quickly after an outage. The self-healing grid can perform risk assessments based on real-time measurements, and, amazingly, it will possess the ability to identify the equipment, power plants, and lines most likely to fail. This smartening-up of the power grid would in real time analyze the overall grid health, identify the warnings signs that could result in grid failure, and identify the need for any urgent repairs or other action to take.

This new, more virtuous power grid will "talk" with local and remote devices designed to help analyze faults, identify areas where voltage is low or where power quality is poor, and uncover where potential system overloads and/or other unstable grid conditions may lurk.

The second of our seven valuable virtues of the new modern grid is that it will motivate consumers to actively participate in the power equation. It will also include them in the grid operations. I am not talking about having everyone don a tool belt and go fix their local power cable if one should fall. Rather, the active participation of consumers in the electricity markets will take the form of new, well-informed power users who can modify their power consumption based on the balancing of their demands and the electric system's capability to meet those demands.

This is, in part, about what are called *demand-response* (DR) programs designed to empower consumers with greater choice in their energy purchases. The ability to reduce or shift peak demand energy by charging more for power used during peak hours will permit utilities companies to minimize capital expenditures and operating expenses while also providing substantial environmental benefits by reducing line losses and the operation of inefficient peak-energy usage power plants.

Our third modern grid virtue is its resistance to attacks. In today's world, security and the threat of terrorism is something that, sadly, must be taken into account when talking about a twenty-first-century power grid. This new security requirement begs for a system-wide solution that will reduce physical and cyber vulnerabilities and recovers one that can bounce right back quickly with minimal power-flow interruptions.

Virtue number four of the modern grid is its ability to provide the level of power quality desired by information-age consumers. New power quality standards will balance load sensitivity with delivered power quality at a reasonable price. The twenty-first-century modern grid will supply varying grades of power quality at different pricing levels, so consumers can get the kind of power quality they need at the price they want.

The fifth virtue is the modern grid's capacity to accommodate all types of power generation and storage options. This new grid will seamlessly integrate many types of electrical power, from traditional fossil fuel sources to green sources such as solar and wind power. It would handle various forms of power storage systems and other sources of on site, or distributed power systems such as fuel cells or hybrid batteries (described in Chapter 10). This ability of the modern grid to accommodate all types of power will make it much easier and much more profitable for commercial power users to install their own generation and electric storage facilities.

The sixth virtuous element of the modern grid is its ability to enable power markets to flourish. The more open a market, the more able it is to expose and shed its inherent inefficiencies. The modern grid will allow market participation through increased transmission paths, aggregated demand response initiatives, and the placement of energy resources—including storage—within a more reliable distribution system that is closer to the consumer.

This new modernized grid will expand markets and bring together more buyers and more sellers. This greater competition and new demand-response pricing model, along with real-time power usage information, will help mitigate demand, drive lower-cost solutions to market, and spur new technology development.

The final modern grid virtue will be its capacity to optimize the grid's assets, allowing it to operate more efficiently. Asset management and operation of the grid will be fine-tuned to deliver what's needed at the lowest possible cost. This does not imply that assets will be driven to their limits continuously, but rather that they will be managed to efficiently deliver what is needed when it is needed.

To accomplish this, advanced *information technologies* (IT) will need to provide a vast amount of data and information that will be integrated with existing enterprise-wide systems. This new data, combined with new IT, will significantly enhance the grid's ability to optimize operations and maintenance processes.

As you can see, the seven valuable virtues of the new, modern power grid are indeed encouraging. The problem is that most of these visionary elements are not currently in practice. Why not, you ask? Well, the answer is a lack of information. You see, in order to make nearly all seven virtues a reality, we have to be able to monitor what the grid is actually doing.

Right now, what the modern grid really lacks is the widespread collection and use of one key ingredient. That ingredient is intelligent systems designed to provide the grid the information it needs to react accordingly.

Enter the age of smart meters.

Meters for the New Millennium

In the late sixteenth century the great advocate of science, philosopher Sir Francis Bacon made the now-famous proclamation that "Knowledge is power." If he could see for himself just how great the scientific knowledge of the twenty-first century is, he'd be a very happy man.

More importantly, however, is putting Bacon's proclamation to the test with respect to the development of the new, modern power grid. You see, the backbone of all of the NETL's visionary goals for the new power grid is information. That information can be garnered only by what's known as smart meters.

These smart meters let utilities collect the information they need so they can get a detailed picture of what's actually taking place on the power grid. All of the things we've discussed so far in this chapter—visionary goals like enhanced grid reliability, greater grid security; a more economic grid, a more efficient and more environmentally friendly grid—have at their very core the requirement of better, more precise, and more accurate information-gathering systems.

This information can be garnered through the widespread use of smart meters.

What Are Smart Meters?

Smart meters can generally be defined as digital devices that collect and transmit data about power usage and other aspects of the power grid back to those who actually operate the grid. I know you are familiar with the old electromechanical electricity meters that measure your monthly energy consumption. These meters have been around for decades, and they require a utility company employee to actually physically come out to your home or business and read the meter to see how much energy you've used that month.

Obviously, this old-school method of finding out about energy usage isn't going to provide anything like the real-time intelligence a smart meter is going to provide. With smart meters, the power company can see not only how much energy a customer is using, but they can see when that energy is being used at any given time.

Information from smart meters is collected in a number of ways, all of which are electronic and do not require that monthly visit from a power company employee. The reduction of manpower needed to read the meters is reason enough for migrating to smart meters. Wireless Internet transmission, radio frequency, broadband over power lines and power line carriers are all methods for retrieving data from smart meters. Which collection method a utility uses depends on its location and other factors, but what's important to understand here is that the information gathered is leaps and bound more precise and more actionable than the old-school or "nonsmart" meter system.

Knowing when customers are using power allows the demand-response pricing model we mentioned earlier to take place. Having smart meters in place throughout the power grid will enable accurate collection of data such as what areas of the power grid are over-stressed, and what areas are likely susceptible to possible outages because of their heavy usage. Also, the real-time data acquired by smart meters can help with utility load forecasting and the related reduction of excess capacity.

The Growth Potential for Smart Meters

In order to achieve all of the objectives of the modern grid, we are going to have to see a widespread adoption of smart meters throughout the United States and the rest of the world. Fortunately for investors in the best smart meter companies, the demand wave for smart meters is just beginning to hit the shore.

In the United States the market penetration rate for smart meters is about 20 percent. Worldwide market penetration for smart meters is just about 15 percent. That means that 80 percent of U.S. meters are old-school electromechanical. Worldwide, we are talking about 85 percent electromechanical metering. With the total number of electric meters estimated to be about 1.2 billion, that's a whole lot of new meters needed to get the power grid into the digital age.

Even if the dream of a completely intelligent, modern power grid takes years to achieve, the market for smart meters is there, and it's likely to keep growing over the next decade and beyond. But who are the players in this industry, and where can you make green from the greening of the power grid? Let's find out.

The Smart Meter Players

The smart meter market has a couple of very big fish, and for the most part, these fish are pure plays in the smart meter segment. The biggest and, in my opinion, best company in the space is Itron Inc. (Nasdaq: ITRI).

Itron is the leading provider of smart meters for electric, gas, and water utilities. In this chapter we've focused on the power grid and its use of smart meters, but the natural gas and water utility industries also use smart meters to help better manage their operations, and Itron is the firm that's making all three of these industries smarter. With over 50 percent market share in electric smart meter segment in the United States and Canada, Itron is the "game-over dominator" in the smart meter space. With over 3,000 customers worldwide, and tens of millions of smart meters operating throughout the globe, Itron is definitely one to watch in the smart meter space.

Another big fish in the smart meter pond is EnerNOC, Inc. (Nasdaq: ENOC). The company provides demand response and energy management solutions for commercial, institutional, and industrial customers as well as electric power grid operators and utilities. In September 2007 the company entered into a five-year agreement to provide demand-response services to one of the nation's largest public utilities, Southern California Edison.

ESCO Technologies (NYSE: ESE) is another solid player in the smart meter world. The company is a diversified manufacturer that focuses on filtration and fluid flow, communications, and testing equipment, along with making hardware and software to support advanced metering applications. In December 2007 ESCO Technologies jumped on the wave of interest from utilities in building smart grids with its $319 million acquisition of Doble Engineering, which makes diagnostic test solutions for the electric utility industry.

Cooper Industries, Ltd. (NYSE: CBE) is a diversified company that's also entered the smart meter market via its acquisition of Cannon Technologies in August 2006. The company now provides the utility industry with power load management tools and services that help manage peak loads and that improve system reliability.

Comverge, Inc. (Nasdaq: COMV) provides peaking and base load capacity solutions to electric utilities, grid operators, and associated electricity markets, primarily in North America. Comverge's Smart Grid Solutions Group develops and delivers demand-response smart metering services and hardware. Its products include digital control units, and a microprocessor-driven solution for load management control that's installed on large energy-consuming devices and controls the cycling and operation of those devices.

Adopting the Information Solution

A general acceptance by power companies and an increasingly informed power-consuming public that our existing power grid is going to need a makeover is becoming a reality. That reality will continue to drive utilities to purchase more and more smart meters, and that increased smart grid adoption will mean a lot of growth for the aforementioned companies in the space.

Much like the transformation in the water sector, the transformation of the power grid into a more efficient—and ultimately a greener—enterprise can be made possible only via sophisticated information technologies like smart meters.

But information technology related to power and power efficiency isn't the only area where IT can play a big role in the greening of our world. In the next chapter I'll show you how information technology departments are going green via virtualization, and how we can make more than just a virtual pile of green by locating the best of the best in the sector.

CHAPTER 7

Eco-Efficient IT

THE NERDS ARE TURNING GREEN

Everything which one invents is true, be sure of it.
—Gustave Flaubert

When you think of the information technology industry, the first thought that comes to your mind is usually not "green." In fact, let's be honest, the first thought that comes to many peoples' minds when they think about those *über*smart guys in the IT department is "nerd."

If you are an IT industry professional, please don't get too bent out of shape at my comments. Let me state here for the record that I use the term "nerd" with the utmost respect and admiration. Without your ingenuity, resourcefulness, and problem-solving abilities, the corporate world would be a whole lot less productive, and way less efficient.

Indeed, the knack for making our world more efficient is what I like most about innovations in IT. In this chapter we are going to look closely at one of the best trends toward efficiency in the IT world. The best part of this trend is that not only does it make computers and computer networks more efficient, it also makes the world a lot greener place. And, from my point of view, the really great part about this trend is that it can help us make money.

Oh, I almost forgot, that trend is called *virtualization*.

The central idea behind virtualization, or more specifically virtualization software, is to in effect turn a single computer server into the equivalent of multiple machines. This move toward virtual computer networks enables companies to save money on the hardware and electricity needed to keep their data centers humming. Virtualization also makes it easier to recover information after computers crash, as all data is stored in real time and off of desktop PCs.

One reason I am so fond of what I call the *virtualization wave* is its incredible potential for growth. According to our ChangeWave Research estimates, server virtualization software sales alone are expected to grow from about $1 billion in 2007 to $5 billion in annual sales by 2011. Computer industry estimates for spending on virtualization software and its supporting services are likely to swell from $6.5 billion in 2006 to more than $15 billion worldwide in 2011. Billions more will likely be spent on compatible hardware and equipment.

This trend toward virtualization is something ChangeWave Research has been watching for some time. It's telling that throughout the past several years, our surveys of IT industry professionals have found an extremely high level of satisfaction among companies deploying virtualization strategies, with nearly 90 percent of software industry professionals reporting they were satisfied with their virtualization program.

But before I get too ahead of myself and start talking about this new way to go green courtesy of the IT department, I want to make sure you understand what virtualization really is, how it works, and why it's so important. I think then you'll realize why I am so fond of the virtualization trend—or as I affectionately call it, *eco-efficient IT.*

What Is Virtualization?

Virtualization is a software technology that is rapidly transforming the IT landscape and fundamentally changing the way that people compute. Today's x86 computer hardware was originally designed to run only a single operating system and a single application. But with virtualization, the monogamy between operating system and application has been broken for good.

Now it's possible to run multiple operating systems and multiple applications on the same computer at the same time, thereby increasing the utilization and flexibility of the hardware. Or to put it another way, your one computer can now perform the work of many.

How Does Virtualization Work?

Put in its most basic terms, virtualization lets you transform hardware into software. By employing virtualization software on a computer, you "virtualize" the hardware resources of that computer, including the CPU, RAM, hard disk, and network controller. This allows the user to create a fully functional virtual machine that can run its own operating system and applications just like a regular computer.

Multiple virtual machines can share hardware resources without interfering with each other so that the user can safely run several operating systems and applications at the same time on a single computer.

Virtualization software makers design their product to be installed directly on the computer hardware or on a host operating system. This software creates virtual machines and contains a virtual machine monitor or *hypervisor* that allocates hardware resources dynamically and transparently so that multiple operating systems can run concurrently on a single physical computer.

Why Virtualize?

Based on the explanation I've given, I think you may agree that virtualization is a very cool technology, but why are companies in such a hurry to implement the virtualization IT model? Or, to put it in cruder terms, what's in it for them?

The main reason why virtualization is being adopted by so many large companies is cost. Virtualization software cuts down on IT costs while increasing the efficiency, utilization and flexibility of existing computer hardware.

According to virtualization software maker VMware, Inc. (NYSE: VMW), which we'll be learning much more about momentarily, here are the top five reasons why companies should adopt virtualization.

1. *Server Consolidation and Infrastructure Optimization.* Virtualization makes it possible to achieve significantly higher resource utilization by pooling common infrastructure resources and breaking the legacy "one application to one server" model.

2. *Physical Infrastructure Cost Reduction.* With virtualization, you can reduce the number of servers and related IT hardware in the data center. This leads to reductions in real estate, power, and cooling requirements, resulting in significantly lower IT costs.
3. *Improved Operational Flexibility and Responsiveness.* Virtualization offers a new way of managing IT infrastructure and can help IT administrators spend less time on repetitive tasks such as provisioning, configuration, monitoring, and maintenance.
4. *Increased Application Availability and Improved Business Continuity.* Eliminate planned downtime and recover quickly from unplanned outages with the ability to securely back up and migrate entire virtual environments with no interruption in service.
5. *Improved Desktop Manageability and Security.* Deploy, manage, and monitor secure desktop environments that end users can access locally or remotely, with or without a network connection, on almost any standard desktop, laptop, or tablet PC.

Each of these five is a great reason to go virtual and, judging by the growing demand for virtualization software, it seems like much of the corporate world concurs with VMware's assessment.

The bottom line here is that a mass move to virtualization could save companies millions of dollars each year, and I think it can become the dominant data center technology within the next two to three years.

How much money can companies save with virtualization? Well, according to industry estimates, a company currently operating 250 dual-core servers can save $4 million over the next three years by adopting virtualization technology. Yes, that's what I call a lot of green.

Now considering that there are currently about 25 million x86-based physical servers out there along with about 500 million desktop PCs, and that only about 5 percent of those servers have been virtualized, I think you can see why there's a lot of room to run for virtualization software makers.

Indeed, what I call the virtualization wave—server virtualization, desktop virtualization, and application virtualization—is just in its infancy. And with the cost savings from the product amounting to millions of dollars for heavy IT users, I see it as one of those no-brainer decisions for corporate IT department managers.

Now I know what you are thinking about now. Toby, this sounds great, but what's the relationship between virtualization software and being green other than it's a good sector to make money in?

Let me explain.

Saving Kilowatts Equals Saving Money

Virtualization is proving to be a cost-effective solution for nearly every kind of firm that utilizes IT systems on any kind of large scale. With virtualization software, companies can make better use of servers and data centers, where a big portion of that equipment is currently underutilized.

But perhaps the real reason why virtualization is included in this book is the tremendous energy savings companies can get by implementing virtualization software. High-tech, database, and other information-intensive companies that need to employ massive data centers are the real beneficiaries here. These massive data centers are notorious for wasting energy. This waste hasn't gone unnoticed by the IT industry. In fact, there is now a movement under way that is being characterized as the "greening of data centers."

As you now know, the central idea of virtualization software is to turn a single computer network server into the equivalent of multiple machines, enabling companies to save money on the hardware and electricity needed to keep their data centers operating.

With virtualization software, an organization's IT infrastructure can reduce its energy consumption by allowing its computer applications to run on fewer physical servers. This reduction of physical servers also reduces power and cooling requirements. This cost savings from energy consumption can be significant. At a savings of approximately $500 to $600 per server, per year, you don't have to be a mathematician or an accountant to know that if you have hundreds or even thousands of servers, you are going to save a lot of money on your power bill.

Compounding the need for virtualization and its power-saving properties is the reality of just how power-hungry modern servers have become. While a typical server in the year 2000 consumed only 100 watts of power, the average server today consumes at least four times that amount. Combined with rising energy costs and increased server density, the growth of data center energy spending could far outpace the rate at which IT budgets grow, leaving less money for other vital IT initiatives and projects.

If you're not aware of the enormous energy costs associated with IT infrastructure, the following industry estimates will likely surprise you:

- Energy costs may increase from 10 percent of IT budgets in 2007 to more than 50 percent in the next few years.
- Servers use about 30 percent of their peak electricity consumption while sitting idle.
- The cost to power servers will exceed the cost of the equipment itself in just a few years.
- Data center energy usage can be 100 times higher than that of a typical commercial building.
- The total power and cooling bill for servers in the United States is estimated to be approximately $14 billion a year. If the current trends persist, the bill is going to rise to $50 billion by the end of the decade.

As you can see, the case for virtualization among corporate IT departments is very sound indeed. An even sounder case can be made that individual investors should consider owning the best companies in the virtualization space.

Virtually the Best

I've mentioned this company already, but virtualization software maker VMware is the undisputed heavyweight champion of virtualization software makers. The company's virtualization solutions enable organizations to aggregate all of their servers, storage infrastructure, and networks into "pools" of capacity, permitting resources to be allocated as needed. The software allows IT departments to optimize server and hardware capacity and lower related costs for storage, power consumption, and hardware outlays.

Based on our findings from a series of ChangeWave Alliance software surveys, VMware is indeed the acknowledged leader in this space. The company's market dominance can be seen in a May 2008 survey of software industry professionals who make software buying decisions for their company.

In Figure 7.1 we can see that VMware has strengthened its domination over the virtualization software market, with its market share among Alliance respondents rising 12 percentage points since the previous January measure.

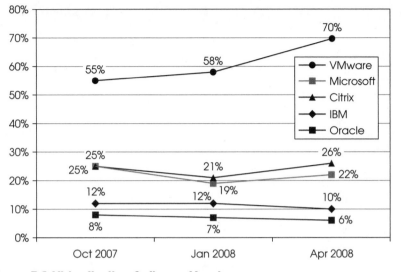

Figure 7.1 Virtualization Software Vendors
Source: ChangeWave Research.

None of VMware's other major competitors have exhibited any-thing like the company's explosive growth. And who are those other companies? Citrix Systems (Nasdaq: CTXS) is an up and coming virtualization software maker trying to dethrone VMware. Another rival getting into the virtualization market place is the biggest soft-ware maker of them all, Microsoft (Nasdaq: MSFT).

Traditionally, Microsoft has always thrown its money and intellectual capital toward developing software products in high-demand areas. This time Mister Softie has a long way to go before it can really start competing with VMware. Still, Microsoft is always a potent rival, and their sheer size enables them to make a go of it no matter how specialized a software market may be.

Having acknowledged Microsoft's potential footprint, VMware is the best of the virtualization stocks out there, and it has the best short- and long-term market prospects. I base this assessment on the intelligence gathered from that May 2008 survey.

In that survey we asked Alliance members about which virtualiza-tion vendors they are planning to purchase or upgrade virtuali-zation software or services from over the next six months. VMware once again reigned supreme over its competition. Here we saw VMware with better than a fourfold lead in planned purchases over its next closest competitor, Microsoft.

Virtualization's "Continuous High Availability"

At a fall 2007 VMware conference in San Francisco, California, chief scientist and cofounder Mendel Rosenblum demoed an impressive step toward raising the high-availability capabilities of virtualization technology.

Rosenblum termed the future of virtualization, "continuous high availability."

He demonstrated this principle with two servers running Microsoft Exchange Server software being replicated in real time from one virtualization host to another. The primary server on stage was running the equivalent of 50 end users simultaneously using Microsoft Outlook. The server's ongoing activity was being mirrored on a secondary server, which received a live stream of events as they were entered into the log of the virtual machine on the first server.

Using VMware's management software, Virtual Infrastructure 3, he unplugged the primary machine, and the second detected a failure and shifted handling the users to the secondary server.

Because the secondary server was already receiving a stream of log events, it could pick up at the precise point where the other had left off. The pause between one virtual machine stopping and the secondary server's virtual machine starting was only about one second.

"Ultimately, virtualization will bring about a vision that server makers years ago presented—a dynamically adjusting, self-managing data center," said Rosenblum.

Although this bleeding edge technology isn't yet on the market, it's clear that VMware is serious about rewriting the history of virtualization.

This shows me that VMware remains the clear leader, with a skyrocketing current market share and extremely strong planned purchasing momentum going forward. The best thing about VMware is that it's still early in the game for virtualization. There are many catalysts on the horizon for virtualization software's widespread deployment, including increased OEM channel distribution, broader adoption in the enterprise software segment and even use in other technologies beyond servers.

Eco-Efficient IT Is the Future

As technologies like virtualization succeed in saving heavy power users money on their energy bills, we're likely to see a lot more innovation designed to make computers, servers, and other IT industry tools more eco-efficient. This is great for the IT industry, great for easing the total demands on an already stressed-out power grid, and it represents a great opportunity for investors looking to profit from the greening of the IT department.

Hey, who said the nerds aren't green?

If you think that virtualization is a cool feat of design and ingenuity, wait until you read about the extreme engineering taking place in our next chapter, which is all about high-tech, biodegradable "green" plastics.

Green Plastics

CLEANING UP SOCIETY'S LEGACY

Science, my lad, is made up of mistakes, but they are mistakes which it is useful to make, because they lead little by little to the truth.

—Jules Verne

When you think about the legacy you'll leave for the next generation, what comes to your mind first? Your answer is likely to be different from mine or just about anyone else's, but one thought I bet didn't come to your mind is *garbage*.

That's right, garbage, as in what we toss away as a society each day, week, month, and year, could turn out to be our most permanent legacy. Why? Well, because a good percentage of our garbage is comprised of the roughly 1 billion tons of plastic produced since 1950. This plastic has the pernicious habit of staying true to form for a very long time, and that means it will likely be around for the next several centuries. Much of this plastic ends up in the world's landfills, and there it sits undisturbed by its environment.

You see, unlike biodegradable waste, nature does not know how to "eat" plastic. Plastic in most of its forms is built to last. The long-lasting characteristic of plastic is one of its many virtues, and certainly, the invention of plastics was one of the greatest developments of the twentieth century. Much like the electrification of the

United States, the advent and widespread use of plastics has been a virtual godsend that's made all of our lives infinitely better.

But as it is with just about anything in life, the good always comes with a little bit of bad. In the case of plastics, the bad is that (1) it poses a problem for waste disposal, and (2) traditional plastics are made from petroleum and other nonrenewable feedstock. This second point is crucial for our purposes, as one of our goals is to be greener in all kinds of areas, including a reduction in the consumption of petroleum-based goods. One way to get greener is to find ways of making our plastics from renewable, non-fossil-fuel sources, and that's where green plastics come in.

The Rise of Green Plastics

Today, most plastics are made from nonrenewable resources such as petroleum feedstock. As you've seen early on in this book, nonrenewable sources like petroleum have their own set of virtues and vices, but it's the vices of rising costs and CO_2 emissions—along with the aforementioned waste issue—that are fueling the trend toward green plastics.

According to industry estimates, more than 300 billion tons of plastics are produced worldwide every year. Today, plastics are so ubiquitous that we don't even think twice about them. In fact, I'd venture a guess and say that most people can't even imagine a time when plastics weren't around. As the world's industrialized population gets larger, and as more and more people in the developing world use more and more plastics, the negatives associated with traditional plastics are bound to increase. Pollution concerns and the rising cost of petroleum will no doubt force industry to come up with new, innovative ways to confront the situation—and one of those ways is through green plastics.

Green plastics, or *bioplastics* as they are sometimes called, are plastics specifically engineered from plant material. This new generation of plastics is made primarily from renewable, agricultural feedstocks. One reason for the renewed interest in green plastics in recent years is the availability and relatively low cost of these feedstock materials compared to $100-plus-per-barrel oil. And while green plastics are gradually replacing plastics made from petroleum, they currently comprise only a small portion of the total plastics made each year.

I think the small market share that green plastics currently occupies means a big opportunity for the best companies in the space, especially as petroleum prices soar and as a the world becomes more attuned toward the virtues of being green. Already, the green plastics sector is growing about 20 percent to 30 percent a year, and that's the kind of growth in an industry I like to see when considering what areas of the market to invest in.

What Are Green Plastics?

Like all forms of plastics, green plastics are composed of a polymers, combined with plasticizers and other assorted additives. But what makes green plastics different from traditional plastics is that they are (1) made of renewable ingredients, (2) biodegradable, and (3) processed in an environmentally friendly way. The importance of this third consideration is probably the hardest to quantify, but for our purposes we can say that green plastics largely consist of a combination of these three basic features.

On a more basic level, the polymers used in the making of the plastic are of biological origin. These polymers are aptly called *biopolymers*. Your basic carbohydrates and proteins are examples of biopolymers. Many biopolymers are already being produced commercially on large scales, although most are not created specifically for the production of plastics. And what are these biopolymers?

There are a variety of biopolymers that can act as feedstock for the bioplastics industry. Among the most popular are cellulose; starch, found in corn, potatoes, wheat, and other plants; collagen; gelatin; soy protein; and even polyesters produced by bacteria are all being produced for commercial, industrial biotech purposes.

A number of other natural materials can be made into polymers that are biodegradable. Lactic acid is now commercially produced on large scales through the fermentation of sugar feedstocks obtained from sugar beets or sugar cane, or from the conversion of starch from corn, potato peels, or other starch source. This lactic acid can be polymerized to produce polylactic acid, or PLA.

Triglycerides can also be polymerized. Triglycerides make up a large part of the storage lipids in animal and plant cells. Each year, billions of pounds of vegetable oils are produced worldwide, mainly from soybean, flax, and rapeseed. Triglycerides are yet another promising raw material for use in the production of green plastics.

These natural raw materials are abundant, renewable, and biodegradable, making them attractive feedstocks for the green plastics industry. Starch-based bioplastics are important not only because starch is the least expensive biopolymer but because it can be processed by all of the methods used for synthetic polymers, like film extrusion and injection molding.

PLA has become a big commercial polymer. The polymer's physical characteristics make it useful for recyclable and biodegradable packaging. Beverage bottles, cups, candy wrappers, and a variety of other food-related applications are well suited for PLA plastics. PLA has also been used for food service ware, lawn and food waste bags, coatings for paper and cardboard, and fibers for clothing, carpets, sheets and towels, and wall coverings. This all-purpose green plastic has also been used in biomedical applications for things like sutures and prosthetic materials.

In the early part of the twenty-first century, PLA emerged as the was the dominant bioplastics technology due in large part to another major player in the bioplastics industry, NatureWorks, which is owned jointly by privately held agricultural giant Cargill, and Japanese chemical company Teijin Ltd.

NatureWorks' PLA plastic is used to pack vegetables, salad greens, and cut fruit sold at retailers like Wal-Mart (NYSE: WMT) and Kroger (NYSE: KR). It also can be found in packaging for Green Mountain Coffee Roasters (Nasdaq: GMCR) coffees, and even in sheets sold at Target (NYSE: TGT) and J.C. Penney (NYSE: JCP). You may not be aware of it, but chances are you've already used bioplastics many, many times without ever knowing it.

Triglycerides are also being used in commercial green plastics. When combined with glass fiber reinforcement, they can be made into long-lasting durable materials with applications in the manufacture of agricultural equipment, the automotive industry and construction.

The Why and Who of Green Plastics

As you can see, there are a lot of interesting solutions and options when it comes to green plastics. I've mentioned just a few of these options, as a complete treatment of all the various types of bioplastics is well beyond the scope of this book. But what is well within our scope is learning why green plastics are likely to be so important in the next few years, and even the next few decades, to come.

My read as to the "why" question is that there is now a realization among the consuming public that we should develop alternatives to traditional plastics. The thinking here is that reducing our consumption of traditional, petroleum-based plastics will help reduce our dependence on fossil fuels and lessen our ecological footprint—or to put it another way, more green plastics make a safer, greener world.

I love this idea, especially given the high cost of oil. But the question is: Can it be done? It's not enough to know that we want to do something, or that something makes sense technologically. The reality is that going green must be both a logical and a profitable proposition. Fortunately, there are companies out there concocting new, innovative ways of producing very sophisticated green plastics.

Perhaps the most interesting of these bioplastics companies is Metabolix (Nasdaq: MBLX). This biotechnology company is at the forefront when it comes to providing alternatives to petrochemical-based plastics. In the 1980s, Metabolix's founders Oliver Peoples and Anthony Sinskey demonstrated an enzyme's ability to integrate into microscopic "biofactories" capable of manufacturing polymers such as *polyhydroxyalkanoates,* or PHAs.

PHAs are linear polyesters produced in nature by bacterial fermentation of sugar or lipids. In a controlled laboratory environment these biofactories combine carbon dioxide, water, and sunlight to create a biodegradable, renewable alternative to petroleum-based plastics.

In 2006, Metabolix formed Telles, a 50–50 joint venture with agribusiness giant Archer Daniels Midland (NYSE: ADM), to commercialize the production of the company's Mirel line of bioplastics. Made by microbial fermentation of sugars such as corn sugar or cane sugar or vegetable oils, Mirel bioplastics are both sustainable and totally biodegradable alternatives to petroleum-based plastics. Telles is now building its first commercial-scale plant in Clinton, Iowa. This plant is slated to start up sometime late 2008, and is expected to produce Mirel at an annual rate of 110 million pounds.

Like PLA-based bioplastics, Metabolix's Mirel can be used as an alternative to petroleum-based plastic in a wide variety of conversion processes. Injection molding, paper coating, cast film and sheet, blown film, and thermoforming can all be used with Mirel. Metabolix is currently working with dozens of prospective customers on more than 60 applications, including consumer products, packaging, single use disposables, and products used in agriculture and erosion control.

Perhaps the best part of Metabolix, at least for someone like me, who views the world through green-tinted investing glasses, is that Metabolix represents the best pure-play company in the bioplastics business. Yes, you can invest in Archer Daniels Midland and get some tangential exposure to the growth of the green plastics market, but that exposure will be dwarfed by the company's huge agricultural business. That business may indeed be a good one to own at certain times, but if you are investing to take advantage of the specific growth in bioplastics, Metabolix is a much better option than ADM.

If you're like me, you are always on the lookout for good small and even microcap companies on the verge of some potentially big growth. In the bioplastics space, one company that fits that bill is Cereplast (OTC: CERP). Founded in 2001, the company develops bio-based resin products.

Cereplast's product line-up consists of two proprietary products: Cereplast Compostables and Cereplast Hybrid Resins. The Compostables consist of biodegradable plastic alternatives derived from starch-based feedstock such as potatoes, corn and wheat. The hybrid resin is identical, except that it is a 50–50 mixture of starches and petroleum. Cereplast is definitely a small company to watch in the bioplastics space.

A Question of Cost and Market Adoption

Bioplastics certainly are a good idea intellectually, but do they make sense economically? Can bioplastics such as PHA and PLA compete with petroleum-based plastics in terms of cost? Thanks to rising oil prices and advances in bioplastic production processes, the net cost of PHAs and PLAs is now well within striking distance of being cost competitive with its petro-brethren.

The interesting aspect of the cost issue is that given the corporate climate in favor of a greener world, the opportunity for bioplastics to displace conventional plastics hinges in part on the premium, if any, that customers are willing to pay for green plastics over petroleum-based plastics. As I just mentioned, given the high price of oil, the choice between green and traditional plastics could soon be a moot point. Nevertheless, at this time there is still the reality that petroleum-based plastics are less expensive than bioplastics.

So, besides costs, what other drivers exist to enable widespread market adoption of bioplastics? In my view, bioplastics will be adopted en masse when the market realizes that product performance is equal to traditional petroleum-based plastics—and that you get tremendous environmental benefits with bioplastics versus traditional plastics.

Finally, never discount the power of government to create demand via regulatory action. Over the past decade, the regulatory tide has been turning in favor of bioplastics. Several U.S. states have required plastic six-pack beverage rings to be photodegradable, and many new federal procurement programs have designated bioplastics as their preferred choice in areas such as adhesives, insulating foam, construction panels, films, carpets, glass cleaners, greases, and metalworking fluids. I think it's safe to say that increased government intervention and a regulatory push toward bioplastics are highly probable, especially given the newfound awareness of all things green.

Just a Drop in the Bio Bucket

You've just seen how one area traditionally dominated by fossil fuels is moving toward biologic alternatives. But this move in the plastics area, while significant, is just a drop in the bio bucket when it comes to an industry that's really all about fossil fuels—namely, petroleum products used to power the internal combustion engines of the world's cars, trucks, motorcycle, and everything else that requires a tank of gas.

In our next chapter we'll look at the biofuels market to see what issues are driving this large, sometimes controversial, sometimes erratic, and potentially very profitable market sector.

A Brief History of Bioplastics

The use of natural polymers, while new in terms of modern green plastics, is not really a new idea.

Natural resins such as amber, shellac, and gutta percha have been used throughout history, including during Roman times and the Middle Ages. Native Americans were said to have developed

(Continues)

(Continued)

and refined techniques for making ladles and spoons from animal horns long before they had any contact with Europeans.

Commercialization of bioplastics actually began in the middle of the nineteenth century. The American inventor, John Wesley Hyatt, Jr., was looking for a substitute for ivory in the manufacture of billiard balls, and in 1869 patented a cellulose derivative for coating nonivory billiard balls. Hyatt continued his work with cellulose, and later developed celluloid, the first widely used plastic. Yes, this is the same celluloid widely known for its use in photographic and movie film.

Plastics changed dramatically in the early 1900s, as petroleum emerged as a source of fuel and of chemicals. Early bioplastics were displaced by plastics made from synthetic polymers. World War II brought about a large increase in plastics production, and that growth continues to this day.

In the 1920s Henry Ford experimented with using soybeans in the manufacture of automobiles. Soy plastics were used to make steering wheels, interior trim, and dashboard panels. After a while, Ford gave his engineers the go-ahead to produce a complete prototype "plastic car." Always the master publicist, Ford exhibited the prototype with great fanfare in 1941, but by the end of the year was no longer publicizing the "plastic car." Because of World War II, the company focuses on armament work, which took precedent over nearly everything else. Of course, today, plastic parts are ubiquitous within the auto industry.

In the twenty-first century, demand for materials like plastics is continually growing and shows no sign of abatement. Be it in the traditional petroleum-based form or in the new green form, the world is going to continue demanding plastics of all sorts, and that translates into great opportunity for investors who know how to pick the best plastics players.

9

Fill 'Er Up with Biofuels

GROWING YOUR OWN OCTANE

A person with a new idea is a crank until the idea succeeds.
—Mark Twain

You've just seen how plastics are going biological in a big way. Now let's look at a trend with the potential to make a much bigger impact on the green marketplace—the move toward biological transportation fuels, or simply *biofuels.*

I've already mentioned my affinity for the smell of ethanol in Chapter 3 on clean transportation. That discussion concentrated on the vehicles designed to be cleaner and greener modes of transportation. And while innovations such as hybrid sedans and battery-operated roadsters are sexy ideas, there is a more intermediate step toward greener transportation, and that step is the widespread use of biofuels.

Biofuels are, simply put, any fuel derived from biologic materials such as crops or crop waste products, wood, plant oils, and other plant matter. Corn and soybeans are examples of crops being grown specifically for conversion into biofuels. Other materials such as sugars and switchgrass also are being grown specifically for fuel production.

How can this be? How do we, in effect, grow our own octane? Well, the energy stored in biomass—which is really just energy captured from the sun and stored in the plant material—can be accessed by turning these raw bio materials into a usable source of fuel that can power an internal combustion engine. Via biochemical or thermochemical processes, scientists have created alternatives to fossil fuels such as ethanol, cellulosic ethanol, biodiesel, and methanol.

When you talk about biofuels, biodiesel and ethanol are really the two biggies. Biodiesel, which is produced from plant oils, is a clean-burning alternative fuel produced from domestic, renewable resources such as new and used vegetable oils and animal fats. Not surprisingly, biodiesel is a popular diesel fuel substitute in areas where diesel engines are heavily used. Europe, for example, has a lot of diesel engine vehicles, especially compared to the United States, so use of biodiesel in Europe is much more common there. But by far the most widely used, most controversial, and most investable of the biofuels is ethanol.

Also called ethyl alcohol or grain alcohol, ethanol can either be used as a stand-alone alternative to gasoline, or it can be blended with fossil fuels and used as an octane-boosting, pollution-reducing additive. Most ethanol—especially the variety grown in America—is produced from the starch contained in grains such as corn, grain sorghum, and wheat. Through a fermentation and distillation process similar to the process used to make adult beverages, grains are converted into starch, and that starch gets converted into sugars. Those sugars are then converted into ethyl alcohol or ethanol.

Mixing ethanol with gasoline is both a key way to reduce the consumption of petroleum fuels and a good way to reduce air pollution. Most American vehicles can run on an ethanol/gasoline concoction called E10, a mixture of 10 percent ethanol and 90 percent gasoline. E85, a mixture of 85 percent ethanol and 15 percent gasoline, is another popular form of ethanol. Unfortunately, E85 cannot be used in traditional vehicles due to the corrosive effects of the high alcohol content on traditional internal combustion engines. *Flex fuel vehicles* (FFVs) have engines modified to accept higher concentrations of ethanol, and thus can run any mixture of gasoline or ethanol with up to the 85 percent ethanol threshold.

I mentioned in Chapter 3 how the American Le Mans Series Corvette Racing team is powered by E85 ethanol, but they aren't the only ultra-high-performance auto racing team to be powered with biofuels. The world of open-wheel racing also has embraced ethanol, as the Indy Racing League uses 100 percent ethanol to power up their mighty horsepower engines. Use of ethanol in auto racing has dispelled any myth that ethanol can't provide high-performance enthusiasts the power they crave. Unfortunately, there are a whole lot of other, more difficult issues surrounding ethanol than just placating those speed freaks out there.

Ethanol: The Good, the Bad, and the Ugly

Like so many aspects of the Green Revolution, there are good, bad, and even some downright ugly aspects to the use of biofuels in general, and ethanol in particular. The good are the advantages of ethanol, and the concomitant gains investors can make by choosing the best companies in the ethanol and biofuels space. The bad are the disadvantages of ethanol use, and the ugly is the very serious issue of global food shortages caused by the increased use of high-value corn crops for ethanol production.

In terms of the advantages of biofuels, the list is long and the prospects are very encouraging. The first, most obvious, and perhaps most important advantage of ethanol and other biofuels is that they are renewable. Unlike petroleum-based fossil fuels, which are finite, hard to extract, and often located in remote and politically tenuous regions of the world, ethanol production is a homegrown proposition. To get more ethanol all we have to do is plant more seed, grow more feedstocks, harvest more biomass, and fire up more distilleries.

Another big advantage of ethanol is that it's a greener fuel than gasoline, meaning it produces fewer *greenhouse gases* (GHGs) than petroleum-based fuels. Today, on a life cycle basis, ethanol produced from corn results in about a 20 percent reduction in GHG emissions relative to gasoline. As the efficiency of FFV and other ethanol-capable internal combustion engines increases, the reduction in GHGs is going to continue getting better and better.

Still another advantage of ethanol is the economic effect it represents to a country's agricultural region. For countries such as the United States that possess vast amounts of farmland capable of growing the feedstock necessary for mass ethanol production, the widespread adoption of ethanol would be—and has already been—extremely powerful. From an energy security standpoint, the move to ethanol makes enormous sense. If you're a country like the

United States, why would you choose to send dollars to oil-rich Arab nations when you can derive the same benefits from fuel grown in your own backyard?

As for the disadvantages of ethanol, the list here is also long. In some cases the disadvantages are downright scary. First on the list of downsides comes from the green purists, who say that no matter how much cleaner biofuels are than fossil fuels, they still support the idea of an internal combustion engine. In other words, you're still burning organic matter in order to extract the energy from it. That burning of matter has the inevitable consequence of creating CO_2 emissions. Therefore, you cannot get to a complete state of green bliss regardless of how clean your fuel source is. And while I agree that there is no getting around the fact that burning organic matter causes CO_2 emissions, certainly biofuels are a step in the right direction if your primary goals are energy security and reduced GHG production.

Other disadvantages of ethanol in its purer, E85 form are the relative lack of FFVs on the road and the concomitant lack of service stations offering E85. In some ways there's a chicken-and-egg situation going on here. Before consumers opt for FFVs there needs to be more E85 stations, but there won't be more E85 stations until there are more FFVs. Fair enough in theory, until you realize that FFVs can use either gasoline, E10, or E85.

I think the real issue when it comes to E85 is a lack of available delivery infrastructure. In order for service stations to become E85 capable, they must install expensive equipment such as new underground storage tanks and new pumps. With little overwhelming consumer demand for E85, the impetus for service station owners just isn't there. Also, many independently owned service stations are under contract with oil companies to sell only their products, and the last time I looked most oil companies weren't jumping up for joy at the prospect of selling E85 in place of gasoline.

Additional disadvantages of ethanol are that in its corn-derived form, it's not a particularly efficient method of extracting energy. Although ethanol has a positive energy balance, that is to say, the energy content of ethanol is greater than the fossil energy used to produce it, that energy balance isn't nearly as good as the energy bang for the buck you get with gasoline. Also, because of its high alcohol content, ethanol cannot be transported through existing oil and gas pipelines. It must be shipped to destinations via railcar or truck. This need for additional transportation methods adds to the overall cost of using ethanol.

Now we've come to what I think is the ugly disadvantage of corn-based ethanol—the rising cost of food, and what's been described as a global food shortage crisis brought about in part by redirection of corn from food production to ethanol production. In a scathing *Wall Street Journal* editorial published May 7, 2008, titled, "The Biofuels Backlash," the newspaper cited chief economist Joseph Glauber of the USDA, whom they described as among "Big Ethanol's best friends in Washington," and his assignment of blame on biofuels for the increasing prices on corn and soybeans.

Indeed, there has been a backlash of sorts against biofuels, particularly because of increased food prices. The fact is that rising demand for ethanol will likely continue causing a rise in corn prices, which will cause the price of food to rise because corn is a central component in the human food chain. The key to solving this problem is to find ethanol feedstocks that aren't derived from substances that are central components in the human food chain. Enter cellulosic ethanol.

Cellulosic Ethanol

All plants contain the cellulosic materials cellulose and hemicellulose. These complex polymers form the structure of plant stalks, leaves, tree trunks, branches, and husks. Cellulosic feedstocks contain sugars within the cellulose and hemicellulose. Like corn sugars, the cellulosic sugars can be converted into ethanol. The problem here is that it's a much more difficult proposition. Cellulose tends to resist being broken down into its component sugars. Hemicellulose is a bit easier to break down, but the problem with hemicellulose is that the sugars you are left with are difficult to ferment.

The technical challenges of developing cellulosic ethanol on a mass scale that is economically competitive with corn ethanol have been the focus of much research over the years. And while there has been good progress made, the fact is there are no commercial cellulosic plants currently in operation. I suspect that will change in the coming years, but when this will actually happen is still speculation.

According to a February 2008 ChangeWave Research survey of industry professionals working in biofuels and related alternative energy industries, there is likely to be a dramatic expansion in total

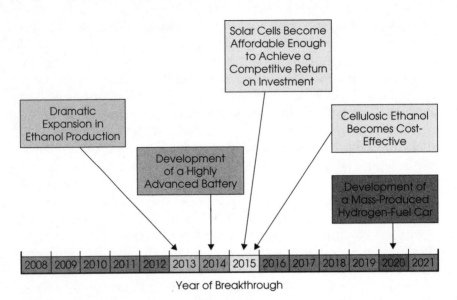

Year of Breakthrough

Figure 9.1   Future Industry Breakthroughs
Source: ChangeWave Research.

ethanol production through 2013. However, the survey found that cellulosic ethanol would not become cost competitive with corn ethanol until 2015. Figure 9.1 shows where ethanol and cellulosic ethanol innovations sit compared to ChangeWave Alliance expectations of where future alternative energy breakthroughs will likely occur.

Still, I think that the research and development and government push toward cellulosic ethanol will continue because the feedstocks used have so many advantages over starch- and sugar-based feedstocks. The first advantage is their sheer abundance. Let's face it; there are a lot more cellulosic plants in the environment than corn fields. If the research can concentrate on developing fast-growing crops like switchgrass as ethanol feedstocks, we'll be able to produce substantially higher amounts of ethanol without encroaching on the world's food supply.

This research into cellulosic ethanol recently got a boost from the farm bill, passed in May 2008 by the U.S. Congress. The bill, which is expected to become law, provides a $1.01-per-gallon production tax credit for cellulosic biofuel through 2012, as well as $320 million in loan guarantees to build refineries. An additional $300 million is slated in the bill for mandatory funding designed to support production of fuels such as cellulosic ethanol. The legislation also includes $70 million in mandatory funding from 2009 through 2012 for farmers to experiment with crops for sustainable biofuels. Those crops include poplar trees and switchgrass.

I think the keys here when talking about cellulosic ethanol are that (1) it will become a necessary alternative to corn ethanol due largely to the "food or fuel" issues with corn; and (2) it is going to take more money and more time to develop mass-produced, economically viable cellulosic ethanol alternatives.

Blame It on Rio

If there is one bright, shining example of how ethanol can be used to replace petroleum fuels, it's the Brazilian model. I know when I put "Brazilian" and "model" in the same sentence, you probably think of Gisele Bundchen or Adriana Lima. And as sexy as those two Brazilian models are, I think what the country has been able to achieve in terms of its energy security via the use of ethanol is equally sexy—well, almost equally sexy.

In 1975 Brazil's government, then a military dictatorship, launched a national ethanol program. Back then, the country imported about 90 percent of its fuel from traditional petroleum exporting countries. To combat this high level of fuel imports, the Brazilian government offered subsidies to sugarcane growers to grow more sugarcane that could then be refined into ethanol. The government also forced service stations in every town of at least 1,500 people to install ethanol pumps. By the early 1980s, almost all new cars sold in Brazil ran on 100 percent ethanol.

As the decade progressed, oil prices fell and Brazil's military dictatorship was replaced with a democratic government. The government removed the sugarcane subsidies paid to farmers, and the result was a shortage of ethanol. Fortunately, the research and development that went into producing ethanol from sugar continued, and when oil prices started to climb again in the late 1990s, Brazil's ethanol producers were right there to provide a sugar-brewed alternative to gasoline. Brazil can now boast near total energy independence, as the country does not need to import any foreign petroleum products.

You may have already deduced that the big difference between Brazilian ethanol and ethanol brewed in the United States is the source of the sugars. In Brazil they use sugarcane as the feedstock for ethanol, while in the United States the primary feedstock is corn. This is easy to do in Brazil, where the country has a whole lot of sugar crops. The great thing about using sugar crops instead of corn to make ethanol is that it is cheaper to produce and it yields a lot more ethanol than corn.

Now logic might prompt you to conclude that perhaps one way to use more ethanol in the United States would be to import it from Brazil. After all, ethanol from Brazil would cost less and it wouldn't contribute to the rising cost of food the way corn ethanol has. Of course, that kind of logical thinking fails to take into account one little pesky fact—the presence of protectionist tariffs.

In its infinite wisdom, the U.S. government slaps a 54-cent-per-gallon import tax on all ethanol from Brazil. This import tax is designed to protect domestic ethanol producers, which of course produce their ethanol from corn. If the import tariffs on Brazilian ethanol were lifted, the total supply of ethanol in the United States would be much greater and the result would be cheaper ethanol, and by extension, cheaper fuel prices.

I don't think this removal of the ethanol tariff is going to happen anytime soon, if ever, as the farm lobby wields a lot of power on Capitol Hill. As the law is currently written, the 54-cent tariff on ethanol imports expires at the start of 2009, but you can be pretty certain that lawmakers will vote to extend this protectionist tax.

The tariff issue brings up another key part of the overall ethanol equation in the United States. One key reason why there is even any demand at all for ethanol is the government. Here I'm speaking specifically of the mandates and tax credits that essentially brewed up America's demand for ethanol. Let's take a closer look at how government's hand helps create the market for ethanol.

Mandates, Tax Credits, and Tariffs

Ethanol first began significant use in the 1970s as a popular domestic alternative to foreign oil imports in the wake of the Arab oil embargo. That unpleasant and economically costly bit of history really highlighted the growing U.S. dependence on foreign oil, and it was one of the big reasons why ethanol was adopted as a partial gasoline alternative.

Ethanol continued to make a small contribution to energy supplies even during the 1980s, when the price of oil was low.

Throughout the 1990s ethanol grew in use as a gasoline additive because of its value as an oxygenate, which helped gasoline comply with federal clean air laws. When automobile technology evolved to overcome the need for ethanol as a clean air additive, government officials decided they didn't want to put the brakes on the ethanol gravy train.

Lawmakers, along with compliant presidents, decided it was best to mandate ethanol's use as a supplement to gasoline early in this decade, and the amount required by law to be mixed into gasoline has gotten larger ever since.

The latest move toward more government-mandated ethanol use came in December 2007, when the Energy Independence and Security Act of 2007 (EISA) mandated the production of 9 billion gallons of ethanol or other renewable fuels in 2008. That number will gradually increase on an annual basis until it reaches 36 billion gallons in 2022. On top of these production mandates, gasoline refineries will receive a tax break of 51 cents a gallon for blending ethanol as a fuel additive, and corn growers will receive huge government subsidies for producing corn for ethanol production.

The combination of mandated ethanol use, along with tax credits for ethanol producers, subsidies for corn growers, and tariffs on any imported ethanol and you've got yourself a cocktail of government intervention that's made the ethanol industry a bit drunk with investment opportunity.

Investing in Team Ethanol

Normally, if a market is very heavily subsidized, you must be very careful when you make your investment calculations. While I still hold to that general principle, in the case of ethanol, the government-created market, along with surging oil prices, has caused ethanol production to grow rapidly in the United States, where it has more than doubled since the late 1990s. That increase in production doesn't show any signs of slowing anytime soon. As of late 2007 at least 76 new ethanol production projects and 10 existing plant expansions have been announced. Now in the face of this increase in ethanol production and use, how do we as investors take advantage of the ethanol boom?

Now, even with all of these ethanol mandates, total use of ethanol as a percentage of the total U.S. fuel supply is approximately

4 percent—that's all, folks! As we've seen in other parts of this book, the small current market share of a particular green technology is a big reason to rejoice, because it means a lot of potential upside for the best companies in the space. And what are the best companies in the ethanol space?

By far the biggest producer of ethanol is agribusiness giant Archer Daniels Midland (NYSE: ADM). I like ADM as a company, but because of its size and diversification, investing in the shares isn't going to provide you with a good pure-play exposure to the ethanol space. Still, ADM is a very good company with a knack for making big profits and for giving investors a solid return on their equity.

If you are looking for a good pure-play ethanol stock, one option is VeraSun Energy Corporation (NYSE:VSE). The company is the biggest pure-play ethanol producer, and it's been on a furious acquisition spree in recent years in an effort to increase its production capacity. Other pure-play ethanol stocks worthy of consideration are Pacific Ethanol (Nasdaq: PEIX), Aventine Renewable Energy Holdings (NYSE: AVR) and The Andersons Inc. (Nasdaq: ANDE). One interesting, yet quite volatile small-cap ethanol producers is Xethanol Corporation (NYSE: XNL).

All of these pure-play ethanol stocks are subject to a lot of volatility, so investing in the space will be an exercise in good timing and vigilance. One reason why stocks in the space are subject to so much volatility is that their profit margins are largely dependent on the cost of their key raw material—corn. If corn prices are rising, ethanol producer profit margins will decline. It's a simple idea, but a powerful one. And even if ethanol prices are rising, if there is a concomitant rise in the cost of corn, then profit margins for ethanol producers are not going to change for the better.

One strategy that largely avoids this relationship between corn prices and ethanol producer profit margins is to invest in companies that support the ethanol industry. Fertilizer producers and corn seed producers come to mind here. On the fertilizer front, Potash Corp. of Saskatchewan (NYSE: POT) is an excellent company supporting corn growers. Another big supporter of the corn industry is seed producer Monsanto (NYSE: MON). Both of these companies will continue to do well even if the high price of corn hurts ethanol producers.

Bye-Bye Biologics

In this chapter, as well as in the previous chapter, we've seen how biological solutions are being rendered to help make the world a greener place. I think that both bioplastics and biofuels have a bright future as partial solutions to the challenges we face in creating a cleaner future. Having said this, we have to keep in mind that investing in either bioplastics or biofuel companies is a tenuous prospect. But, hey, if green investing were a complete slam dunk proposition, you wouldn't need me to help you understand how to do it.

Now let's say good-bye to biologics and move on to another highly interesting set of solutions to the problem of power generation and power storage. In Chapter 10 it's all about fuel cells and advanced batteries, or what I call the rise of pink bunny power.

CHAPTER 10

Fuel Cells and Advanced Batteries

THE RISE OF PINK BUNNY POWER

Bring in the bottled lightning, a clean tumbler, and a corkscrew.
—Charles Dickens

I t's safe to say Dickens wasn't referring to energy technology when he talked about "bottled lightning," but in the twenty-first century we know that a whole lot of bottled lightning can be uncorked using a variety of sophisticated devices, and two of the most interesting types are fuel cells and advanced batteries.

Before we go on I want you to picture in your mind Energizer Inc.'s (NYSE: ENR) long-time mascot, the Energizer Battery Bunny. In one of Energizer's animated TV commercials, their little pink pika steps in to provide a substitute source of electricity after a big power generation plant malfunctions and sends the city into darkness. The idea here is that a battery can save the day as a backup source to the power grid. And while this idea is largely fiction right now, technology in both the fuel cell and advanced battery market sectors is getting to the point where this pink powerhouse scenario might not be all that far-fetched.

Let's take a look at both fuel cells and advanced batteries to get a sense of the science, market applications, and investment possibilities in each.

Fuel Cells: Hydrogen Anyone?

Does the name William Grove mean anything to you? If you're like me, you probably never heard of Grove until you learned something about the history of fuel cells. You see, Grove was the first person to create a fuel cell, although it wasn't called that back in 1839—over a century and half ago. The *Grove cell,* as it was called then, is really the basis for today's modern fuel cells.

The Grove cell was based on the fact that sending an electric current through water splits the water into its component parts of hydrogen and oxygen. Grove reasoned that if you reversed the reaction and combined hydrogen and oxygen you could produce electricity and water. I know it sounds simple, but often simple ideas are the genesis for huge scientific change.

Now let's fast-forward to the present day, where fuel cells are enjoying a resurgence of sorts with a greener public in search of solutions to the challenges of rising energy prices, our need to increase energy security, and the desire to curtail carbon emissions. Today, modern fuel cells are all about the hydrogen, and what some have called the emergence of the "hydrogen economy." The current iteration of fuel cells work by converting chemical energy into electrical energy, or electricity, with heat and water generated as by-products. No CO_2 emissions or GHGs here, folks. Like internal combustion engines, fuel cells continue to generate power for as long as a fuel is supplied.

Unlike internal combustion engines, where fuels are burnt in order to convert chemical energy into kinetic energy, fuel cells convert fuels directly into electricity via an electrochemical process that does not require combustion. This process is much more efficient at creating electrical power than are engines that have to go through an additional step of converting the kinetic energy into electrical energy.

So, how do fuel cells work? Well, without getting too scientific, here is a basic summary. First, hydrogen molecules enter the fuel cell at the anode, where a chemical reaction strips them of their electrons. The ionized (positively charged) hydrogen atoms pass through an electrolyte membrane. The negatively charged electrons then pass through a wire outside the fuel cell to create an electric current. The electrons and protons mix with air on the cathode to complete the reaction and create water as an exhaust.

This is the basic way a fuel cell works, but when you're talking fuel cells, there are several different kinds. Some fuel cells work at relatively low temperatures (under 300 degrees Fahrenheit), and some operate at extremely high temperature ranges (300 degrees Fahrenheit to 1,800 degrees Fahrenheit). Low-temperature fuel cells have different applications and are better suited to certain tasks than high-temperature fuel cells. One difference between low-temperature fuel cells and high-temperature fuel cells is the high-temperature variety can take advantage of cogeneration, which is just a term for the excess heat produced in the power generation process, to actually help produce even more electricity. Let's look at some of the most common types of fuel cells and see how each can be used.

Fuel Cell Types and Applications

All fuel cells contain either solid or liquid electrolytes that are sandwiched between two electrodes. Different types of fuel cells can be characterized by their particular electrolyte. The main types of fuel cells are: polymer electrolyte membrane or *proton exchange membrane* (PEM); *direct methanol fuel cells* (DMFCs); *solid oxide fuel cells* (SOFCs); *molten carbonate fuel cells* (MCFCs); and *alkaline fuel cells* (AFCs).

By far the most common type of fuel cell is the PEM. This fuel cell uses pure hydrogen as fuel, which is electrochemically combined with oxygen to produce electricity. PEM fuel cells operate in the low temperature ranges and are primarily used for transportation, backup power, and portable applications. Direct methanol fuel cells also are low temperature, and, like PEMs, they are suitable for small portable applications, and even micro applications. The difference between DMFCs and PEM cells is DMFCs convert liquid methanol, rather than hydrogen, into electricity.

Solid oxide fuel cells and molten carbonate fuel cells both operate at high temperatures. SOFCs do not require pure hydrogen and can operate with hydrocarbons such as natural gas as a fuel. Given their operating characteristics, SOFCs are generally associated with fixed combined heat and power generation projects. MCFCs are similar to SOFCs, but the major difference is MCFCs are based on molten carbon salts and have a significantly more complex design which limits their use to large-scale power generation.

Finally, there's alkaline fuel cells. AFCs operate at low temperature, but do not require membranes; however, they still require the use of pure hydrogen as fuel. These fuel cells were the power choice for many early NASA projects.

As you can see, there are many types of fuel cells. The main reason for this variety has to do with suitability of applications. Some fuel cells just work better than others for certain types of power usage. What are those applications? Well, PEM fuel cells are currently used in automotive applications as car engine replacements. PEM cells are usually the first thing most people think about when they think about a fuel cell. I think a functional, low-cost hydrogen-fuelled electric engine could be a really significant step toward reducing carbon emissions and gaining more energy security, but right now issues like cost and durability are keeping the mass adoption of a fuel cell-centric transportation industry from becoming a reality. PEM fuel cells also are used for *uninterruptible power source* (UPS) applications, and for uses such as powering onboard vehicle electronics.

Direct methanol fuel cells (DMFCs) have found their niche applications in armed conflict. More specifically, DMFCs have a wide variety of military uses. Modern warfare has created a new modern warrior, and that warrior carries a lot of electronics with him to the battlefield. Powering those electronics means carrying a lot of battery power—and a lot of heavy batteries—onto the battlefield. By carrying only lighter, more powerful DMFC fuel cells, the modern-day soldier can have all the power he needs without the burden of carrying the excess weight of traditional batteries. Other, more mundane uses for DMFC fuel cells are everyday devices such as cell phones, smart phones, and laptop computers.

Molten carbon fuel cells are, as previously mentioned, the logical choice for large-scale power generation. Because they can operate on less-than pure hydrogen sources, and because they are more efficient due to cogeneration, they can be used to generate a whole lot of backup power. I am talking megawatt-sized power, or power that's enough to keep hospitals, factories, hotels, and other large facilities humming in the event of a power grid failure. MCFCs also may be used to provide backup power for large power-generation facilities in the event of a widespread grid outage. You see, I told you that Energizer Bunny commercial wasn't that far-fetched.

Big Costs, Big Benefits

There are a lot of benefits to fuel cells, but there are also a few big drawbacks. The biggest drawback is cost. According to the Department of Energy, fuel cells currently cost approximately $3,000 per kilowatt output. Many experts believe this is a very optimistic, low-ball cost estimate. The real cost could be anywhere between 30 percent and 70 percent more. But even the Department of Energy says that for fuel cells to become cost competitive with traditional forms of power generation, the cost per kilowatt output must come down to the $1,000 level.

The current high cost of fuel cells is due to many factors. Material such as polymers used for PEM fuel cells and specialty ceramic powders used in solid oxide fuel cells come at a considerable cost. Fuel, in the form of hydrogen, is plentiful on earth. The only problem is that hydrogen is always locked up in the form of water and hydrocarbons. Pure hydrogen isn't found anywhere on earth, so to get the pure hydrogen needed for fuel cells requires costly synthesis from its "locked-up" form into its pure form.

Low-temperature fuel cells require precious metals catalysts to ensure a successful electrochemical reaction. The current industry standard metal choice for this catalyst is platinum. Anyone who has shopped for a wedding ring or other fashionable jewelry can tell you about the high cost of platinum in recent years, and like jewelry shoppers, fuel cell manufacturers aren't immune to the trend of rising platinum prices. Finally, fuel cells require high levels of engineering to produce a successful product. Given the current economies of scale in the industry, production costs will likely remain an issue for some time. So much for the big costs involved in fuel cells; now let's look at the big benefits.

The biggest benefit to fuel cells is their clean, or green, attributes. No CO_2, no GHGs, just water vapor. You have to love that. Even when fuel cells are powered by fossil fuels as opposed to pure hydrogen, they produce far less pollution than conventional power technologies. Fuel cells are also very efficient. They extract more energy from their fuel source than conventional power technologies. Also, there are no moving parts in a fuel cell stack, and that means there are no mechanical inefficiencies where energy can be lost. The lack of moving parts makes fuel cells virtually silent and vibration free. The lack of both noise and vibration makes fuel cells well suited to indoor applications.

The absence of moving parts means that fuel cell technologies also are extremely reliable, especially when compared to traditional combustion engines. High-quality power also is a big benefit of fuel cells. The DC power generated from fuel cells is ideal for modern electrical applications such as sensitive electronics and medical equipment. Yet another benefit of fuel cells is their lack of need to be recharged. As long as there's fuel available, the fuel cell will keep going, and going, and going.

For me, one of the biggest benefits to fuel cells is that some-day they could help us become independent from the traditional, centralized energy infrastructure. Rather than get all of our electricity from the power grid, why not generate that power at home with our own fuel cells? Mass use of fuel cells could free us from our tether with national power grids, reducing the damage done by blackouts and brownouts. Fuel cells could also help us get a lot greener, as widespread home and industrial use would reduce overall GHG emissions, and widespread transportation use would help us become more energy independent.

Powering Your Portfolio with Fuel Cells

Widespread use of fuel cells may be only a future reality, but what isn't a future reality is the numerous companies in the fuel cell space. There currently are many publicly traded companies working on specific fuel cell technologies, and many of these companies are worthy of consideration in any green investing portfolio.

The biggest fuel cell maker, and the most well known, is Ballard Power Systems, Inc. (Nasdaq: BLDP). The company was one of the first to make PEM fuel cells for the transportation industry, and it has made alliances with several big automakers such as Ford (NYSE: F) and Daimler AG (NYSE: DAI). Plug Power (Nasdaq: PLUG) is another well known fuel cell maker. Like Ballard, the company's focus has been on PEM fuel cells. The company makes the GenCore line of uninterrupted power supply products for use in the utility sector and other infrastructure markets. Plug Power also makes transportation fuel cells designed for light industrial vehicles.

Industrial giant United Technologies Corporation (NYSE: UTX) has a division called International Fuel Cells, and while United Technologies (UT) has some heavy capital available to put into research and development, it's not the best way to play the fuel cell market due to the tiny amount of business that it's fuel cell division does in relation to UT's other industrial businesses. If you're looking for a pure play in the space, UT is definitely not it.

There are a few other solid pure plays in the fuel cell sector, each with varying specialties. Medis Technologies (Nasdaq: MDTL) makes microfuel cells for portable consumer electronics market. Its 24/7 Power Pack product is a disposable power source capable of providing direct power or multiple recharges to portable electronic devices such as mobile handsets, smart phones, MP3 players, and other handheld electronic devices. The company also develops fuel cells for laptop computers as well as stationary fuel cells for small-scale emergency backup power.

If you are looking to play the hydrogen production angle, then you should check out Distributed Energy Systems (OTC: DESCQ). Not only does it make PEM fuel cells for backup power systems, the firm also develops fuel cells for those on-the-move modern warriors in the military. The company also develops hydrogen fueling systems designed to "fill up" depleted fuel cells.

Perhaps the most interesting way of powering your portfolio with fuel cells is via a company appropriately called FuelCell Energy (Nasdaq: FCEL). These guys make MCFC, high-temperature fuel cells for use as backup power sources for power generation stations. In early 2007 the company established a 10-year manufacturing and distribution agreement with POSCO Power to provide fuel cells to power generation plants in South Korea. FuelCell Energy's high-temperature fuel cells are designed to run on natural gas or other hydrocarbons, which allow them to avert the high cost of acquiring pure hydrogen. I joked about this last year when I started following FuelCell Energy, but I am about ready to put a miniplant in my house in suburban Maryland. I swear it will pay for itself in 8 to 10 years or less, purely on electricity bill savings.

Advanced Batteries

While fuel cells certainly are the most interesting aspect of pink bunny power, I shouldn't omit advancements in battery technology.

As you know from Chapter 3, advanced battery technology is currently being used to power up hybrid vehicles.

Nickel-metal hydride (NiMH) batteries are a staple in the hybrid vehicle market, but this advanced battery technology is also being employed for use in stationary backup power systems and the consumer electronics market. NiMH batteries have the advantage of being much more energy dense than traditional battery technologies such as lead acid and *nickel-cadmium* (NiCd).

The market for NiMH batteries is likely to grow over the next several years and beyond, due in part to the growth in the hybrid vehicle market, but also due to growth in the consumer electronics segment. When it comes to hybrid batteries, there is no better company to own than Energy Conversion Devices (Nasdaq: ENER). The company is a virtual patent library for many advanced battery technologies, and its diversified intellectual property portfolio makes it one to consider when investing in the advanced battery space.

One of the newest trends in the advanced battery market is the growing use of *ultracapacitors* and *supercapacitors*. Basically, ultracapacitors and supercapacitors store electricity by physically separating positive and negative charges. This differs from regular batteries that separate positive and negative charges chemically. The charge held by ultracapacitors and supercapacitors is like the static electricity that can build up on a balloon, but is much greater thanks to the very high surface area of their interior materials.

Ultracapacitors and supercapacitors can provide up to 100 times more instantaneous power than traditional batteries, and they generate less overall heat. Like fuel cells, ultracapacitors and supercapacitors have no moving parts, which make them very reliable. It also makes them last very long. With no moving parts, they also have a very long life span. The downside to these advanced batteries is that they store a smaller amount of energy than a battery does, and hence they must be larger in order to get the same amount of energy as a comparable battery source.

Investing in this new, advanced battery market via publicly traded companies is a limited proposition. The one name in the space worth looking into is Maxwell Technologies, Inc. (Nasdaq: MXWL). Maxwell develops, manufactures, and sells the BOOSTCAP line of ultracapacitors for industrial, transportation, telecommunications, and a variety of other advanced battery applications.

The ultracapacitor and supercapacitor market is expected to grow quite rapidly over the next few years, so this is one advanced battery market segment you need to keep your green eye on.

Another area to keep your green eye on isn't all that new. In fact, generating power from this source has been blowing around for about 2,000 years. I am talking here about wind power, and it's the focus of Chapter 11.

Wind Power

HARNESSING NATURE'S BREATH

A modern fleet of ships does not so much make use of the sea as exploit a highway.

—Joseph Conrad

Humans have been harnessing nature's breath for centuries. As far back as ancient Egypt, wind-propelled boats traveled along the Nile River. Windmills first appeared in Persia in the seventh century, and soon after were used in China and Europe. Of course, these windmills weren't used to help reduce the carbon footprint of their respective societies. The use of wind power helped make everyday tasks such as grinding grain into flour much easier, and hence the economic savings of labor that could be allocated to more productive tasks.

As history continued on its technologically driven march, societies found new ways to put reins on the wind. The most famous of these wind-riding societies were the eleventh-century Dutch, who figured out how to use windmills to help reengineer the lakes and marshes along the Rhine River delta.

Fast-forward about 1,000 years and the discussion of how best to harness nature's breath rages on. The only difference between the discussions back then and now is that we want to know what companies are best positioned to help us harness the wind in our investment portfolio. And by the way, the technological issues and challenges are a bit different now.

I'll discuss the issues swirling around modern-day wind power in a moment. Before exiting this trip down the historical wind tunnel, it might be helpful to look at one more bit of nostalgia. In the late nineteenth century, larger windmills, or wind turbines, came into use in Denmark to generate electrical power. But with the industrialization of the twentieth century and the electrification of Europe and the United States, such early attempts at wind power generation went into decline.

Wind power's appeal came back into the public eye from time to time, especially when the price of oil and other fossil fuels spiked. In the 1970s the Arab oil embargo got people to think seriously about wind power. The real commitment toward this source of ultraclean energy, however, never really caught on until recently. In the first decade of the twenty-first century, the whole equation for wind power has changed.

Blowin' Up the Energy Charts

In May 2008 the U.S. Department of Energy (DOE) released the 2007 edition of its *Annual Report on U.S. Wind Power Installation, Cost, and Performance Trends.* This comprehensive overview of developments in the U.S. wind power market found that U.S. wind power capacity increased by 46 percent in 2007. The report also revealed that $9 billion was invested in U.S. wind plants during the year.

Now, if you think the growth in wind power in 2007 was an anomaly, think again. It was the third consecutive year that U.S. wind power grabbed the top spot as the fastest growing wind power market in the world. The report also showed that wind is on a path to becoming a significant contributor to the U.S. power mix, with wind projects accounting for 35 percent of all new U.S. electric generating capacity in 2007.

The DOE's report goes on to analyze developments in the wind market, including trends in wind installations, turbine size and prices, project costs, and cost comparisons between wind power and conventional generation. It also describes developer consolidation trends, project financing structures, and trends among the major wind power purchasers.

Along with being the fastest-growing wind market worldwide, market growth in the United States is helping to spur manufacturing investments in the wind sector. Several major foreign wind turbine manufacturers either opened or announced new U.S. wind turbine manufacturing plants in 2007. The report found that both new and existing U.S.-based wind turbine manufacturers also either initiated or scaled up production in 2007.

The report also found that wind turbine prices and installed project costs have risen since 2002. Turbine price increases have been driven by factors such as a weak U.S. dollar, higher prices for materials and energy inputs, and shortages in certain turbine components. I'll have more to say on this subject in a moment.

Finally, the report showed that wind power is now providing good value in wholesale power markets. Despite rising project costs, wind power has consistently been priced at, or below, the average price of wholesale-priced conventional electricity.

All these findings are good news for wind-generated electric power in general, and particularly for the wind power industry in the United States. But the United States is still just a small slice of the overall wind power market. Germany, Spain, France, and the United Kingdom have a lot of installed wind power generating capacity, and the emerging giants of China and India are ramping up their capacity at a feverish pace.

Why is virtually the whole world trying to harness nature's breath? The answer lies in the many advantages to wind power relative to the minor, yet still important disadvantages.

The Good and the Bad of Blowin' in the Wind

The wind never dies.

Because winds are created by the uneven heating of the earth's atmosphere by the sun, irregularities of the Earth's surface, and the rotation of the Earth, there will always be wind, which means there will always be a source of free and inexhaustible energy. This free fuel is similar to the free fuel we get with solar; and really all we are doing with both wind power and solar power is taking the modeling clay nature gives us and sculpting it into usable forms of clean energy.

The main advantage to wind power generation is the free, and 100 percent clean, fuel source. Wind energy does not emit CO_2 or other GHGs the way fossil fuel electricity generation plants do. Because wind energy is a local proposition, it's a domestic source of energy for any country where wind supplies are abundant. In the United States there are many regions conducive to wind power generation, and that means a lot of opportunity to power much of the country.

Wind energy also is one of the lowest-priced renewable energy technologies available today, costing between 4 and 6 cents per kilowatt-hour, according to the DOE. The cost here varies due to, among other factors, the source of the wind and the cost of building and operating the wind power generation facility.

Another advantage of wind power is that wind turbines can be built on farms or ranches, which benefits the economy in rural areas. It makes sense, too, as most of the best wind sites are found in rural areas. Also, because wind turbines are big structures that require a lot of space between them, the land where a wind farm sits can be used for multiple purposes. Farmers and ranchers can continue to work the land literally between and below wind turbines. The added benefit to farmers and ranchers is that wind power plant owners will actually pay them to use their land. For a land owner, this practice is akin to having a great big house and then renting one of the rooms.

Hey, who even needs land? Wind power can be harnessed at sea, where the winds are actually strong and unencumbered by terrain like buildings, trees, or mountains. This offshore capability of wind, that is to say, the ability to build offshore wind turbines, is another advantage to wind power generation.

Despite the advantages of wind power, it does come with a few disadvantages. And like we've seen with other alternative energy sources, cost is once again a big issue. In order to become really attractive, wind power must compete with conventional power generation on a cost basis. Depending on how robust a wind site is, the wind farm may or may not be cost competitive. Even though the cost of wind power has decreased dramatically over the past decade, the start-up technology still requires a higher initial investment than fossil-fueled electrical generation. Adding to this cost equation is the need to build additional power transmission lines, and possibly even infrastructure such as roads to help service remote wind farms.

Another major disadvantage to wind power is intermittency. Although the wind never dies, it doesn't always blow hard enough to turn a wind turbine. Because wind energy cannot be stored without the help of batteries, it is not always capable of generating electric power when that power is needed. Ironically, if the wind blows too hard, power generation can be stymied because wind turbines can be damaged in very high winds. This Goldilocks scenario means that the wind has to blow just right or a wind farm won't be able to generate power.

Also in the disadvantage column are concerns over noise. The sound produced by a wind turbine's rotor blades is a nuisance to some, as are the aesthetics of wind turbines. There is also the issue of ecology as large wind turbines can kill birds that fly into the turbine's rotors. Given these considerations, this technology does have its beauty and poetry as you can see in the box "Desert Inspiration."

Desert Inspiration

I revved the engine on my 1989 Porsche 911 as soon as I saw the huge white posts on the horizon. Appearing like sentinels guarding the entrance to southern California's San Gorgonio Pass, my foot instinctively pushed the throttle down in an effort to get a closer look at these mechanical creatures that appeared as if they were characters from an H.G. Wells novel.

I turned the top down on the Porsche to get an even better, more spectacular view of the towering devices, which I knew to be the large-scale wind turbines that help supply power to the nearby Coachella Valley. Pulling up along a remote road off of Interstate 10 for an up-close inspection, I sat in the car and stared upward at the giant blades silently spinning overhead, their rotor sweep nearly half the length of a football field.

Nearly two decades later I can still remember the sense of awe I felt looking up at those spinning blades. For me, they represent the genius of man's mind in concrete, physical terms. Maybe because I've lived in southern California most of my life my local bias clouds my judgment, but in my opinion there is no better example of how man has learned to reshape the world for his own life-sustaining purposes.

If there is a nobler pursuit for mankind, then I am clearly not aware of it.

—Jim Woods

Turbines at a Glance

Before I get any deeper into the issues surrounding wind power—and how we can profit from investing in the space—I want to cover a few basics of wind turbines. Wind turbines convert the wind's kinetic energy into mechanical power. This mechanical power can then be used for specific tasks. As you have already seen, wind power was used in the past for grinding grain and pumping water out of the Rhine River delta. Today, that mechanical power is harnessed to generate electricity.

How do wind turbines make electricity? Basically, the process is like pressing the rewind button on a fan. Yes, I know fans don't generally have rewind buttons, but play along with me for the illustrative purpose. In the case of a fan, electricity is used to turn the blades of the fan. The turning of the blades then creates the wind. If you reverse the process you get wind turning the blades on the turbine, which then spins a shaft. That shaft is connected to a generator and presto—you've got electricity!

When discussing wind turbines, size truly does matter. The big utility-scale turbines range in size from 100 kilowatts to as large as several megawatts. If you've ever seen one of these large turbines up close, you'll know that it's a very impressive sight. When these larger turbines are grouped together, you have a *wind farm*. The wind farm can then be hooked up to the power grid via transmission lines.

Smaller-scale wind power is usually considered to be below 100 kilowatts. These smaller turbines are used primarily to power homes and small industrial or farming structures. Small wind turbines are often used in conjunction with diesel generators, batteries, and photovoltaic systems. These are called hybrid wind systems, and they're typically used in remote areas that aren't connected to the power grid.

The Breezy Dynamics of Growth

When you are talking about the growth of wind power, you are talking about growth not just in the United States, but also big growth worldwide led by China, India, and Europe. How much growth are we talking about? Well, nobody can say for certain, but I've seen some estimates as high as a fivefold increase in new installed wind power capacity between over the next decade.

According to Danish wind power consultants BTM Consult, global wind power will triple to 287 gigawatts by 2012. A slightly less bullish, yet still very robust global growth forecast comes from the

Brussels-based trade group Global Wind Energy Council (GWEC). The GWEC claims global wind power will rise to 240 gigawatts by 2012. At the end of 2007, the world had total capacity of just about 94 gigawatts.

In March 2008, GWEC upwardly revised its previous growth estimates because of consistent growth in both the United States and China. In fact, the Chinese government just doubled its own forecast for wind power development by 2010. According to BTM Consult, China can increase its wind capacity sevenfold in the next five years, while the United States could reach 60 gigawatts of wind, up from 16 gigawatts today.

What both of these expert forecasts have in common is the notion of a very bright future for the wind power industry. Now our goal is to determine which companies can capitalize on this world-wide trend toward catching the breeze.

Subsidies and Supply Shortages

In the United States—and even more so in other parts of the world—you always have to consider the issue of subsidies. In the case of wind power, the United States subsidy at issue is the Production Tax Credit (PTC). The PTC allows an income tax credit for the production of electricity from qualified wind energy facilities and other sources of renewable energy.

The current value of the credit is 2 cents/kilowatt-hour of electricity produced. The credit was created under the Energy Policy Act of 1992 at the value of 1.5 cents/kilowatt-hour, but that number has since been adjusted annually for inflation. The credit applies to electricity produced by a qualified wind facility placed in service after December 31, 1992, and before January 1, 2009. The PTC is applicable only to utility-scale wind turbines, so you small-fry wind farmers are out of luck.

The current status of the PTC is not guaranteed, however; and, as of mid-2008, it was scheduled to expire on December 31 of that year. Since its establishment in 1992, the PTC has undergone a series of one- and two-year extensions. However, it also has been allowed to lapse in 1999, 2001, and 2003. Understandably, the wind power industry wants the federal government's uninterrupted commitment to the PTC, and while most industry observers think it will be renewed, it's by no means guaranteed.

The important thing to know about the PTC is that helps the wind industry make investment decisions. If you know there will be a tax credit, you'll factor that into your financial analysis. If you don't know for sure you can count on the PTC, then you won't make any business decisions until Congress makes its decision on the PTC. This tenuous status for the PTC has already caused some companies in the industry to hold off on new investment. The good news here is that given the current political winds, which are forcefully in favor of wind energy, I think the passing of a PTC is a very safe bet.

Along with the PTC, another wind industry issue begs for discussion. Given all of the growth in the space worldwide, the industry is suffering from a shortage of wind turbines. That's right, wind turbine makers are having a really tough time keeping up with demand.

Supply chain shortages for wind turbine component parts like gearboxes, bearings, and materials such as carbon fiber have all limited the industry's growth. It's not uncommon for wind farmers to have to wait 18 to 24 months before they can take delivery on a wind turbine order.

Right about now you might be thinking this back-order status for wind turbines bodes well for many companies in the space. To some extent that is true, but the supply chain backlog also is a hindrance to the industry, as it restricts the output of component part makers. Think of the backlog as one giant bottleneck clogging the wind industry's freeways. Traffic jams are rarely good, whether it be on the freeways or in business.

Five "Easy" Steps to Developing a Wind Farm

Think you've got what it takes develop a wind farm? I mean, how hard could it really be? All you have to do is buy some wind turbines and hook them up to a few power lines, right? Well, it's not quite that simple. In fact, it's a mammoth proposition that involves a number of significant challenges, not the least of which are community objections and securing government permits.

Here is what I call the five "easy" steps to developing a wind farm, which, of course, aren't easy at all.

Step 1: Location and Testing. Before a wind farm can be developed, there has to be a suitable location to put the wind turbines on. As the developer, you'll have to secure the rights to construct and operate the farm on the property, which can be tricky if the property is owned by the government. To make the location a viable option, wind speeds in the area must be tested for about a year to determine if there is sufficient wind flow in the area. Keep in mind that if the location doesn't have enough wind flow, or if there isn't enough wind flow during peak power demand times, you'll have to find a new space.

Step 2: Planning & Permissions. Once you've passed the wind test, it's time to start planning. You'll have to make sure the area has access to the power grid. If it doesn't, you may have to build out the infrastructure in the form of more power lines and/or access roads for service and repair vehicles. Assuming you've gotten this far, you'll then have to get permission from local governments to actually build the farm. This step kills off many a wind farm project, because there is always a contingent of folks in any area who just don't want a wind farm built in their backyard.

Step 3: Get Your Agreements and Financing. If you can climb up steps 1 and 2, you're then faced with the prospect of securing what's called a *power purchase agreement,* which can differ greatly depending on where the farm is located and who your customer is. Once you've got the agreement, you'll need to find the financing, which usually comes in the form of nonrecourse project funding—meaning your project will be placed up as collateral for your loan.

Step 4: Furnish the Farm. Here is a big potential bottleneck in getting your farm up and running. Due to high demand and shortages of component parts and materials, the delivery time once you've placed your order for a wind turbine is running somewhere between 18 and 24 months, so you'd better not be the impatient type.

Step 5: Build and Operate. If you get through the first four steps, all you have to do now is build the wind farm. Oh, and finally, you have to operate the facility or at least package it for sale to a willing buyer.

I don't know about you, but I can think of a whole lot easier ways to make a buck.

Investing in Windy Conditions

So, how do you invest to take advantage of the windy conditions in the wind power industry? First off, you must realize that there aren't a whole lot of pure plays in the space. Sure, there are the mega-industrial giants like General Electric (NYSE: GE) and Siemens (NYSE: SI). But as I've pointed out several times in this book, you shouldn't be buying these big industry behemoths for their exposure to alternative energy revenues.

The second obstacle for U.S. investors is that many of the bigger companies in the wind industry are based either in Europe or India. These companies do not trade on U.S. stock exchanges. Yes, you can get exposure to these sectors using exchange-traded funds; but as far as pure play options in the United States the pickings are somewhat slim in number. Nevertheless, this doesn't mean that they are slim in *opportunity*.

If you are a more intrepid investor and don't mind going international with your equity purchases, you might want to consider international wind turbine manufacturer Vestas Wind Systems (CPH: VWS). The Copenhagen-based company is the largest wind turbine manufacturer in the world, with an estimated 23 percent market share worldwide and approximately 35,000 wind turbines installed around the globe.

Spanish company Gamesa Corporacion Technologica (MCE: GAM), India-based firm Suzlon Energy (NSE: SUZLON) and U.K.-based Clipper Windpower (LON: CWP) are other big pure-play international turbine companies. In June 2008 the DOE announced that it had reached an agreement with six of the top turbine makers—including GE, Siemens, Vestas, Clipper, Suzlon, and Gamesa—to promote and develop wind as a power source. The goal of the promotional effort is to have wind power produce 20 percent of America's electricity needs by 2030.

In my view, the turbine makers are not the way to make green in wind industry stocks. I think the better strategy is to find one or two—more if they exist—companies on the cutting edge of the supply chain. One of my favorite pure plays here is carbon fiber materials maker Zoltek Companies (Nasdaq: ZOLT).

Zoltek is the world's leading manufacturer of carbon-fiber material, which is the material of choice for the giant rotor blades found on large-scale wind turbines. The company is the "game-over dominator" in the wind power component space. Zoltek's customers include Vestas and Gamesa, so you know they are playing in the big leagues.

Because carbon fiber is lighter and stronger than steel, and much stronger than fiberglass, it's the material of choice for wind turbine manufacturers. Carbon fiber also is less prone to friction and lasts 10 times as long as fiberglass, which enhances its efficiency as a material for the blades that turn the turbines.

One of the keys to the new efficiencies in wind power today is blade size, and carbon-fiber materials facilitate an increase in blade size of three to four times the size of just a few years ago. Indeed, this is yet another case where size does matter, because more blade equals more turbine-turning power per rotation. A wind turbine with four times the blade area at approximately the same weight can turn a much more powerful turbine and create about four times the power per rotation.

It's the companies providing key market advantages—like enhanced industry efficiency—that tend to outperform the competition over time, and Zoltek is certainly positioning itself as one of the wind industry's best performance enhancers.

Blowing on to Chapter 12

As you've just seen, wind power is a growing industry with quite a bit of market potential. And while the investment options in the space aren't as numerous as some of the other green sectors we've covered, the opportunity and enormous growth potential of wind power makes it a must-watch sector for any green-oriented investor.

Another must-watch sector really isn't a specialized sector per se. Rather, it's a new twist on how to improve old-school power generation sources such as coal and other fossil fuel–powered utilities. I call this trend the New, Old, Green Tech. Read on.

The New, Old Green Tech

CLEANING UP COAL'S ACT

There are mysteries which men can only guess at, which age by age they may solve only in part.

—Bram Stoker, *Dracula*

When you think about old, "dirty" energy technology, what comes to your mind first? I know what comes to my mind first is the face of a seasoned, dust-covered coal miner who has just spent eight hours valiantly extracting the energy-rich rock from below the earth's surface.

Now, I am not going to bash coal in this chapter because I think coal power has been—and will remain—one of the cheapest and most reliable sources of energy in the United States and other coal-rich nations. But, hey, we can all use a little cleaning up from time to time, and coal is no exception.

When it comes to the bang for the energy buck, you can't get too much better than coal. The energy content stored in U.S. coal resources is said to exceed that of the entire world's known recoverable oil. According to the U.S. Department of Energy (DOE), coal supplies more than half the electricity consumed by Americans. There is no denying that coal-fired electric-generating plants are the backbone of America's power generation infrastructure, and all of our green dreams combined will not make that reality go away for what I suspect will be many more decades.

Of course the downside to coal is that when burned, it emits a lot of CO_2. According to the International Energy Agency (IEA), the burning of coal is responsible for approximately 40 percent of the world's CO_2 emissions each year. Burning of petroleum also contributes about 40 percent of CO_2 emission. That means that no matter how much we curtail auto emissions through hybrid and flex-fuel cars, we've also got to tackle the problem of CO_2 from coal. Another downside to coal is the substantial amount of environmental damage done from coal mining, and the human toll taken on coal miners in the form of bodily injury and death in the ultrahazardous occupation.

There have been many theories and a lot of research and development money put into trying to figure out how to make coal a cleaner, greener energy source. Some of the technological solutions, while interesting from a scientific perspective, aren't yet commercially viable. There are, however, some technologies that are viable right now. Of course, there are a few publicly traded companies helping to clean up coal—and there are even some that may help us clean up with green profits.

The Coal, Hard Facts

Here are the cold, hard facts—or in this case, the *coal*, hard facts—that are likely to drive coal consumption higher over the next two decades and beyond. We've got strong energy demand worldwide, record high oil and gas prices, and mounting concerns over energy security all teaming up to create big drivers for sources of nonpetroleum energy. Some of that energy will be generated from alternative sources such as solar and wind, but much more of that energy will be supplied by good old-fashioned coal.

In recent years coal use has climbed in Europe, the United States, and Asia. Approximately 50 coal-fired power plants have been slated for construction over the next five years in the European Union, and in 2007 there were approximately 150 proposals to build new coal-fired power plants in the United States. But that growth is relatively insignificant when you compare it to the growth in China and India. Chindia is now constructing a new coal-fired plant at the rate of about one per week. That's huge.

The fact that coal is becoming a greater and greater source of power generation shouldn't really be a big surprise, especially if you're even the least bit familiar with the literature on this subject. In fact, the IEA has long projected a rise in coal usage based on energy security grounds. And why shouldn't there be an increase in coal use? The IEA says there is at least 200 years' worth of coal reserves in geographically dispersed areas, including big deposits in the United States, Russia, China, and India. The sheer quantity and geographic desirability of coal means it will likely account for more than 25 percent of the world's power generation by 2030.

The relative ubiquity of coal resources in regions of the globe with relative stability compared to the oil-rich Middle East make coal an increasingly attractive option for power generating electrical power. There's also the issue of coal's being a proven technology over many years. There's a long history of coal-fired power generation, which means there won't be any issues with the technology involved.

As mentioned a moment ago, the big disadvantage of coal is that it tops the list of dirtiest carbon-based fuels. Given the overwhelming likelihood of greater coal use over at least the next couple of decades, we have to figure out what can be done to mitigate the negative effects of coal.

Movin' On Up from Low Grade to High Grade

One way to clean up coal's act is to step up from low-grade coal to high-grade coal. What's the difference? Low-grade coal has a higher ash and moisture content than high-grade coal. The low-grade coal doesn't burn as completely as the high-grade variety, and it also emits more pollutants.

What if there were a way to make the low-grade coal burn like high-grade coal? Wouldn't this be one way to help coal clean up its act? Indeed, it would—and there is one company with a proprietary solution that does just that.

The company is Evergreen Energy (NYSE: EEE), and the process they use to help clean up coal is called *K-Fuel*. Evergreen uses heat and pressure to both physically and chemically transform high-moisture, lower-Btu coal into what effectively becomes the more efficient, lower-emission, high-grade variety. The K-Fuel process removes significant amounts of mercury, sulfur dioxide, and nitrogen oxide emitted when burning low-grade coal. It also reduces the CO_2 emissions whenever you burn either low-grade or high-grade coal.

In 2005 Evergreen Energy began production in its 750,000-ton-per-year K-Fuel production facility near Gillette, Wyoming. The company plans to develop and operate K-Fuel production plants both in the United States and internationally, via either wholly owned or joint ventures, and through international licensing to third parties.

According to the company, the K-Fuel process doesn't make coal "clean," but it makes coal cleaner and more efficient. The process can increase coal's heat value by approximately 30 percent to 40 percent, which means 8,000-Btu-per-pound coal becomes 10,500 to 11,000-Btu-per-pound coal. This type of improved efficiency on the coal clean-up front is one big reason to keep your eye on Evergreen Energy.

Scrubbing Coal's Image

More efficient burning coal is great, but how about if the sulfur dioxide and nitrogen oxide emitted when coal burns could be scrubbed away? This would be another way to help coal become a lot greener.

The star here in the "scrubber" market is Fuel Tech (Nasdaq: FTEK). FTEK has developed proprietary air pollution control technologies that utilities and industrial facilities can use to cut nitrogen-oxide (NOx) emissions. While Fuel Tech's NOx system doesn't remove quite as much NOx as some of its competition's products, those more sophisticated systems can cost up to $100 million to install. For many plants, especially older plants or plants in emerging markets, that level of investment is simply not economical.

As of 2007 Fuel Tech's NOx system was installed in more than 400 plants worldwide, including China and India. Its NOx scrubber system is a proven, economical technology with a large, existing installed base. This gives Fuel Tech a significant advantage over any upstart competitor. But the real action could be in the company's Fuel Chem anti-slag/CO_2 reduction.

Fuel Chem involves a proprietary mixture of chemicals essentially designed to cut CO_2 emissions affordably and without dilution of production. Fuel Chem also improves boiler efficiency and cuts sulfur and carbon dioxide emissions. Both segments rely heavily on the company's unique ability to inject chemicals in combustion units, in precise concentrations and locations, to achieve a desired scrubbing effect.

Fuel Chem is a great business because of the "razor-and-blades" business model affiliated with their emissions-reducing installations. Fuel Tech gets to sell chemicals to each site at very high margins. Thus, they become the new "Gillette" of the clean energy business.

The Great Carbon Roundup

I love the term "mitigation strategies." It sounds like a battle plan drawn up by a brilliant military mind. And in a way, what's needed to combat the negative effects of the growing use of coal-fired power plants and their related carbon emissions does indeed amount to a battle plan.

Mitigation strategies such as clean coal technology and *carbon capture and storage* (CCS) are two of the ways the energy industry plans on fighting the CO_2 emissions battle. And while some clean coal technologies from some of the companies discussed in this chapter have been successfully implemented, the widespread commercial and technical viability of CCS is far from being a reality.

Basically, CCS is an attempt to in effect "capture" carbon dioxide emissions generated from either coal or other fossil fuel power plants and "store" it underground instead of releasing it into the atmosphere. The technology for CCS is fairly well developed; however, the long-term storage of CO_2 underground is a relatively untried concept, and as of 2007 there were no large-scale power plants operating with a full carbon capture and storage system.

The potential for CCS as applied to a modern conventional power plant is encouraging. The consensus thinking here is that a power plant could reduce its atmospheric CO_2 emissions by some 80 percent to 90 percent by using CCS. That kind of CO_2 reduction would be wonderful, but unfortunately, there are at least two big obstacles to the widespread implementation of CCS technology—cost and CO_2 storage locations.

Although there are a number of small CCS projects in the United States and Europe, most have suffered from cost overruns. In January 2008, the Department of Energy announced it would withdraw funding from its FutureGen project, an ambitious undertaking that would have built a near zero-emission coal-fired power plant with the capacity to generate 275 megawatts of energy—and capture and store CO_2 underground.

There was a lot of political wrangling involved in the DOE's decision, and as with any political issue there is always the possibility of a different outcome. However, one chief reason cited for pulling FutureGen's plug was cost. The trouble began in December 2007 after the FutureGen Alliance of coal companies and electric utilities announced it had picked Mattoon, Illinois, as the site of the proposed power plant. Later that month, the DOE released a statement reminding the alliance that federal regulators would have to approve any site selection. They also said they were concerned about the projected cost overruns, which were 58 percent higher than the $950 million originally expected.

Cost overruns in a big government project are no big surprise. However, the bottom line with CCS technology is that it is a costly proposition. Some estimates peg the cost of CCS capable power plants at about 10 percent to 20 percent more to build than conventional plants. For most coal-fired plants, the costs of becoming CCS compatible would be unrealistically high.

The other big issue for CCS is storage location. Where do you put tons and tons of CO_2? Geologists have warned that the number of sites that could be considered safe for storage is limited, and some scientists even think CO_2 storage could be extremely dangerous— even more dangerous than storing nuclear waste.

Big Coal Goes Green

You know the tide in coal has turned green when the world's largest coal company makes an undisclosed investment in a clean coal start-up.

In January 2008 privately held GreatPoint Energy announced that it had raised an undisclosed amount of money from Peabody Energy (NYSE: BTU). GreatPoint said it would use the cash to develop its technology at commercial scale. Aside from the minority stake, the companies announced a strategic relationship in which Peabody would supply GreatPoint with coal. The companies also said they were considering developing a joint coal-gasification project using Peabody reserves and land.

Why the move by Peabody? Well, one reason might be the desire to go green for green's sake. Skeptics might say the reason for Peabody's move was to improve their image in the minds of New York State investigators. In September 2007 Peabody was one of five energy firms that New York Attorney General Andrew Cuomo subpoenaed in as part of an investigation into whether planned coal-fired plants' greenhouse gas emissions would result in previously undisclosed financial risks.

In my view the motivation for Peabody's investment in GreatPoint is immaterial. The important thing is that for whatever reason, clean coal companies now realize they need to go green. Be it for environmental or purely public relations reasons, the trend toward greener coal isn't likely to go away anytime soon.

Despite the issue with clean coal and CCS, the reality is that we need to round up CO_2 emissions from coal-fired plants. That reality must be, and indeed will be, acted upon, and that means opportunity for companies that can deliver the right technology at the right price.

A Deeper Shade of Green

As we've just seen, there is a move toward the greening of coal, and there are several green companies working hard to make coal plants cleaner. As the world's appetite for more energy increases, coal will continue to be one of the staples in the world's energy diet.

By investing in companies out front and leading the way toward cleaner coal, you'll be positioned to profit from the energy demand wave as well as one of the biggest waves I've ever seen—the Green Revolution wave.

One big component of this Green Revolution is a change in personal attitudes. People now think being greener equals a more virtuous life, and in the next chapter you'll see how this new green attitude means a lot of new opportunity throughout many different industries.

All this talk about coal and the likelihood of a surge in demand might have you thinking that investing in coal companies might be a way to go directly to the source for energy profits. And while the focus of this book is on all things green, I am not going to deny that "Big Coal" or even "Big Oil" have been solid places to park your money over the past several years.

So, who are the biggest publicly traded coal companies? Peabody Energy (NYSE: BTU) is the big boy on the block, but other big players in the coal industry include Arch Coal (NYSE: ACI), Consol Energy (NYSE: CNX), Massey Energy (NYSE: MEE), Natural Resources Partners (NYSE: NRP), and Yanzhou Coal Mining Co. (NYSE: YZC).

I mention these companies not in the context of investing in just green energy stocks, but with the realization that your first goal as an investor is to make money. If alternative energy stocks are in vogue, then stick with them. If, however, energy stocks are in vogue along with traditional energy stocks, why not add a little bit of tradition to your portfolio?

CHAPTER

Living La Vida Verde

GREEN BUILDINGS, LIGHTING, NATURAL FOODS, AND LIFESTYLES

Each problem that I solved became a rule, which served afterwards to solve other problems.

—Rene Descartes

I t's not easy being green."

Those are the words of that famed Muppet philosopher Kermit the Frog, whose refrain became a phrase burned into the pop culture of the 1970s. A lot has changed since Kermit first uttered his lament. And while the Muppet wasn't referring to the idea of being more eco-aware, nowadays "being green" has taken on a life of its own well beyond anything Kermit could have imagined.

Putting a modern twist on the articulate amphibian's idiom, today we can quite confidently say that it is, in fact, easy being green. Today, being green is all around us. It's in the buildings we live and work in, and the devices that illuminate our world. It's in the foods we eat and clothes we wear. And perhaps more importantly, being green has become a philosophical imperative for many who've chosen to be part of what's sometimes called the "Green Movement."

So, what are the implications of this move toward living *la vida verde*? (That translates as "the green life" for those of you far removed from your high school Spanish.) Well, the answer depends upon your perspective. My perspective—and the perspective of this book—is that of an individual investor. Sure, being green might be a good idea, but as you've seen so far, there's a lot of potential to make money by investing in companies providing green solutions.

I think the move by consumers toward all things green means a continuation of the big boom many companies providing greener goods and services have seen in recent years. In this chapter I'll cover some of the best, most investable areas related to living the green lifestyle. From buildings to bulbs to beverages and much more, living la vida verde might soon be the key to living *la vida rica*.

The Green We Inhabit

Ben Franklin is purported to have uttered the following piece of profundity: "A penny saved is a penny earned." Allow me to borrow from Ben here and say that when it comes to energy, a kilowatt saved is a kilowatt earned. Or, to put it in another way, the cheapest—and greenest—energy is the energy you never have to use. I know this makes sense on the face of it, but how do we get there? How can we take steps in our own lives to use less overall energy? A few answers can be found, quite literally, right in your own home and office.

When it comes to green living, why not start with your residence or your place of employment? Not the location of your home or office, I mean the type of buildings you inhabit. Enter the concept of green buildings. Normally, one does not associate a building with being green, but the wider awareness of all things eco-efficient is causing a paradigm shift in the building industry.

The idea of greater energy efficiency in the structures we inhabit has been around for a long time. However, it wasn't until the early 1990s that the *green building movement* found its official voice. That voice belongs to the U.S. Green Building Council (USGBC), a non-profit organization whose members include companies involved in building and related industries, universities, and government agencies. The goal of the USGBC is to help promote sustainable living through greener building standards. Those greener standards were codified in 2000, when the council developed the Leadership in Energy and Environmental Design, or LEED.

These LEED standards, along with the LEED-certified rating system, were designed to evaluate and judge the green characteristics of any structure. The standards have become the benchmark for evaluating the energy efficiency of structures, as well as the efficiency of their heating, ventilation, and air conditioning systems.

According to the USGBC, in the United States alone buildings account for 70 percent of electricity consumption; 39 percent of energy use; 39 percent of all CO_2 emissions; 40 percent of raw materials use; 30 percent of waste output (136 million tons annually), and 12 percent of all potable water consumption. Improving the energy efficiency—as well as the rest of the above metrics—through strict building standards is the primary goal of the USGBC. And judging by the data, those goals are starting to really catch on.

According the USGBC, there are buildings that meet LEED-certified standards in all 50 states and in 69 countries. As of June 2008, there were 11,921 registered LEED projects, and 1,537 LEED-certified projects. Stunningly, the organization says that every business day $464 million worth of construction registers with LEED. This is some pretty significant growth in the green buildings segment, and it is growth like this that we want to take advantage of by investing in companies benefiting from the green building wave.

One company riding this green building wave is Echelon Corporation (Nasdaq: ELON). The company designs, builds, and sells networks that connect machines and other electronic devices for the purpose of sensing, monitoring, and controlling the world around us. You see, before you can save energy, you've got to know where and when that energy is used, and that means you need some very smart devices that can provide you with the data necessary to do so. As a leader in this field, Echelon's LonWorks platform has become a worldwide standard in the building, industrial, transportation, and home automation markets.

As we saw in Chapter 6, automated meter reading systems, or smart meters, are now starting to replace the old mechanical meter reading systems. But replacing this century-old technology is only the beginning. The future of greener buildings is in what's called energy consumption management. I like to call this *negawatt management*.

The idea behind negawatt management goes back to the concept that a kilowatt saved is a kilowatt earned. Remember that the easiest, fastest, cheapest, and, ultimately, cleanest form of energy is the one that never has to be produced in the first place. Using less of what we have depends on a transformation in power consumption management—that is, *networked energy management*.

With Echolon's LonWorks in place, a factory or other heavy power consumer—even an individual home—can manage their power usage more efficiently. Echolon's products give power users the tools they need to regulate energy usage by controlling air conditioners, refrigeration units, and other large electricity-consuming sources via a sophisticated network of computers, sensors, and wireless technology. Think of LonWorks as a smart meter on steroids, enhancing the performance and efficiency of all power-consuming devices.

Another big player in building efficiency and negawatt management is Johnson Controls (NYSE: JCI). Johnson is the oldest and largest company in this field. According to the company, between 1990 and 2005 their building efficiency solutions saved customers over $32.7 billion in energy costs. The caveat here on Johnson is that they are not a true pure play in the energy efficiency or green buildings segment. Their other businesses are auto parts, including auto batteries and even hybrid batteries. Still, JCI is definitely one company to watch as the green building wave continues barreling toward shore.

By the Dawn's Early Green Light

Perhaps an even better way of negawatt management is to install devices that radically reduce energy consumption when used. Greater efficiency appliances come to mind here, and for sure, the energy saved by more efficient products like air conditioners, refrigerators, dishwashers, and clothes washers and dryers is significant. Unfortunately, the investment options here are severely limited. That's because nearly all the major appliance makers are complying with the U.S. government's voluntary "Energy Star" labeling program. And while it's a good thing that thousands of kilowatts per year will be saved due to more efficient appliances, there really aren't any ways to take advantage of this from an investment perspective.

One area in the home, office, and even literally in the streets—where there is the potential for both significant energy reduction and investment opportunity—is lighting. It's estimated that nearly 25 percent of all energy used in the United States goes toward lighting us all up. If you've ever been to New York City, Chicago, or Las Vegas, the knowledge that it takes a huge amount of energy to light up the country will come as no surprise.

Given the industrialization of the developing nations, and the tremendous shift taking place from the country to the cities in places like China and India, you can bet there's going to be greater and greater consumption of energy for the purpose of lighting up the world. But why, you may ask, does this even matter? Haven't we got a proven technology that's over 100 years old, namely, the incandescent light bulb? Indeed we do, and that's the problem.

You see, traditional incandescent light bulbs are extremely energy inefficient. About 90 percent of the electricity used in light bulbs is radiated away in the form of heat. The light part of the equation gets only a minimal amount of the overall energy involved. Now, if there were a way to make light bulbs more efficient, we could cut down on the total power consumed and by extension cut down on all of the negative aspects of greater power generation such as rising greenhouse gases, rising costs, and diminished energy security.

Thankfully, there are proven technologies that let you see the light without all of the radiant heat runoff. The most common of these technologies employed today is fluorescent bulbs. Although fluorescent bulbs are nothing new, what is new is the *compact fluorescent light bulb* (CFL). These funny-looking, squiggly-shaped light bulbs are now commonplace, and for good reasons.

First, CFLs use a lot less electricity than traditional incandescent bulbs. On average, CFLs use only about 25 percent of the energy required to power up an incandescent. That's a big-time efficiency advantage. The second reason why CFLs are growing in popularity is due to their longevity. These bulbs can last up to eight years with normal usage, which means you won't have to change them out very often—especially when compared to incandescent bulbs.

The downside of CFLs is, for many people, the quality of light generated. Although CFL light has become better over the past several years, there is no doubt that many people still prefer reading by the soft light of an incandescent bulb. Also, CFLs cost a lot more than incandescent bulbs. But given their longevity versus traditional bulbs, and the reduction in energy consumption, the higher costs of CFLs are largely offset.

Once again, however, we have a familiar issue with CFLs. That's the issue of a lack of pure-play investment options in the space. When it comes to CFLs, or even traditional lighting, big boys like General Electric (NYSE: GE), Phillips Electronics (NYSE: PHG), and Siemens (NYSE: SI) are the only real options. And as we've seen so often in this book, the big boys are just too big to be moved by light bulb sales alone.

LED Lighting Leads the Way

Now I come to the part of the *green building wave* that I am really excited about—*light emitting diode* (LED) lighting. I see LED lighting as one of the best opportunities—in terms both of energy conservation and investment opportunity—in this green revolution.

Sometimes referred to as *solid-state lighting,* LED lighting technology creates light with less heat than either incandescent or fluorescent bulbs. And unlike incandescent and fluorescent bulbs, solid-state lighting uses a semiconducting material to convert electricity directly into light. This high-tech approach is known to immensely improve energy efficiency. LED lights are generally three to four times more energy efficient than incandescent bulbs, which means your green home, building, or even local traffic signal—something LED lighting is increasing being used for—is going to be a far smaller drain on the power grid.

The best part of the LED lighting thesis is the pure-play investment options in the space. Once again, I look at the world through green-colored glasses, meaning I am looking to be green both socially and financially. Let's take a look at two standout companies in the efficient lighting space.

The first company doing big things in the space is Cree, Inc. (Nasdaq: CREE). The company develops and manufactures semiconductor materials used for LED lightning. The company's niche is that its semiconductor materials are based on silicon carbide, gallium nitride, silicon, and other related compounds.

If you're familiar with my *ChangeWave Investing* advisory service, you'll know that I've written quite a bit about the "death of the light bulb" in recent years. No company stands to benefit more from what I think will be an inevitable shift away from incandescent bulbs to LED lighting than Cree. The value of Cree's LEDs is their ability to increase energy performance. The company's customer list ranges from innovative lighting fixtures makers to defense-related federal agencies, which gives it broad inroads into many LED markets. Its products include blue, green, and near-ultraviolet LED chips, as well as high-power packaged LEDs.

After years of developing its LED technology and steadily lowering costs, the world is waking up to the virtues of Cree's LED lighting. The signing into law of the Energy Independence and Security Act of 2007 (EISA) will likely be a big boost for Cree, as it contains a provision requiring a phase-in period between 2012 and 2014 of light bulbs that use about 20 percent to 30 percent less energy than most current incandescent bulbs. CFLs and LEDs already meet the new energy consumption standards. Also, several high-profile LED installations in public spaces like New York's George Washington Bridge and Holland Tunnel will help to increase the public's awareness of LED lighting.

The big drawback with mass-market adoption of LED lighting is cost. Just a short time ago the cost of an LED light was about 50 times more than the cost of a power-output incandescent bulb. Of course, LED lights have a much, much longer life span than incandescent bulbs, plus they are ideal for certain types of applications like traffic signals, tunnel lights, and bridge lights because they don't have to be replaced very often.

Another company to keep tabs on has its hands in both the lighting space—although not specifically LED lighting—and the energy efficiency space. The company is Orion Energy Systems (Nasdaq: OESX), and it designs and manufactures energy management systems consisting primarily of energy-efficient lighting and energy monitoring controls. The company offers its Compact Modular lighting system, which operates at lower temperatures than so-called high-intensity discharge fixtures and other legacy lighting fixtures found in so many commercial and industrial facilities.

Orion is the prototypical energy efficiency company, combining deep knowledge in the field with years of hands-on experience at delivering results to major customers. Most of Orion's revenue is generated from the sale of *high-intensity fluorescent* (HIF) lighting systems to commercial and industrial customers. These are usually retrofits that are installed by a company's existing electrical contractor.

Orion's lighting systems generally reduce lighting-related electricity costs by about 50 percent compared to those high-intensity discharge fixtures, while improving the lighting quality and increasing the quantity of light by approximately 50 percent. The company already boasts an impressive customer list, including nearly one-fifth of Fortune 500 companies.

The ChangeWave Alliance on Energy Usage

There's a new standing order in corporate America, and it goes a little something like this: Be much more energy efficient.

The trend toward energy efficiency was made patently clear in a new ChangeWave survey of corporate spending on energy efficient products and technologies. Conducted the week of March 24–28, 2008, the survey of over 1,400 respondents involved in making purchasing decisions for their companies uncovered a renewed emphasis on overall energy usage. The results also showed a concerted effort on the part of companies to buy energy-efficient products and technologies.

The survey showed that more than one in five (22 percent) respondents said their company is *very concerned* about reducing its energy usage. Another one-third (35 percent) say they're *somewhat concerned* about reducing energy usage in general. This elevated level of concern over total energy consumption is leading to a significant shift in corporate energy usage, with over one-quarter (26 percent) of respondents saying their company has used *less* energy than normal over the past six months. Only 16 percent of respondents say they've used *more* energy over said time period.

A key finding in the survey shows that nearly one-quarter (23 percent) of respondents report their company's spending on energy efficiency products and technologies will *increase* over the next six months, nearly three times the percentage that see a *decrease* (8 percent).

Overall, current corporate use of alternative energy technologies is gaining momentum, with 8 percent of respondents saying they use off-the-grid sources to generate power. Going forward, better than one in five (21 percent) say they'll install and make use of alternative power sources within the next five years.

Energy-efficient lighting was the top product/technology companies will be purchasing over the next six months to help improve energy efficiency. Although compact and regular fluorescent lighting maintained the greatest market share in terms of the types of lighting companies purchased over the past six months, LED lighting was the clear momentum leader going forward.

One obstacle to wider adoption of LED lighting is cost. Price is still the key factor in terms of LED lighting, with nearly three quarters (74 percent) of respondents saying their company would consider replacing all of its lighting with LED only if the cost were less than

$5 per bulb. But the survey does clearly show that LED lighting is a prime spending area in the world of corporate energy efficiency.

The bottom line here, according to this survey, is that companies are concerned about their energy consumption, and they are in the market for more energy efficient products. That trend means big opportunity for investors, particularly in the solar and LED lighting markets

Green Movement Market Opportunities

No book on investing in the Green Revolution would be complete without at least a small mention of the investable opportunities related to the Green Movement and what I call the "greening of the global Zeitgeist." This movement epitomizes what many people think of when they picture people who've embraced green lifestyles. The folks in the Green Movement have, to varying degrees, adopted green thinking as a kind of quasi-religious identity. They make value judgments based largely on how their purchasing and lifestyle choices will affect the planet.

I am not criticizing this green orientation, nor am I advocating it as a way to live. What I am pointing out is that the basic ideas of the Green Movement, that is to say, the tendency toward making the green choice in everything from what to wear to what car to drive, what building to live in, and what foods to eat all have ramifications for companies supplying this newfound green demand.

As you may have already figured out, it's not just the hardcore greenies that have the Green Movement mind-set in place when making purchasing decisions. I know that given the choice between a green product and a not-so-green product, I will choose the green product—provided, of course, that it serves my needs equally well, and that it doesn't come at an exorbitant cost.

When it comes to investing in green companies, however, my allegiance is to the monetary style of green. Fortunately, there are some good green-oriented stocks out there that appeal to Green Movement diehards as well as to those who, like me, will opt for the green choice whenever it makes sense.

One area of the Green Movement that elicits a lot of passion among its advocates is organic and natural foods. Some people just won't eat it if it isn't green. There's also a growing contingent of people who just like the idea of all natural and organic foods from a health standpoint. And there are many people—myself included—who just plain like the taste of organic beef, organic coffee, and organic wine.

Where can you find all of these specialty food items in one place? Whole Foods Market (Nasdaq: WFMI). As of May 2008 the company owned and operated 269 natural and organic food grocery stores in the United States, Canada, and the United Kingdom. In addition to being a great place to shop, Whole Foods has just about everything a green appetite desires. And if you are really committed to the Green Movement, you can buy all kinds of products such as nutritional supplements, soaps, household products, and even pet products at its stores. In August 2007, Whole Foods acquired a majority stake in rival grocery chain Wild Oats Markets. The move made Whole Foods the premier pure play in the natural and organic food sector.

Another smaller, yet much more specialized green food company actually has the word "green" in its name. The company is Green Mountain Coffee Roasters (Nasdaq: GMCR), and it specializes in roasting, packaging, and distributing coffee primarily in the northeastern United States. Green Mountain sells approximately 100 whole-bean and ground coffee selections, hot cocoa, teas, and specialty coffees.

The company offers some very specialized coffee choices, including single-origin coffees, estate-grown coffee, certified organic blends, and even Fair Trade Certified coffees. In 2007 the company's shares benefited from a big trend toward green coffee consumption, a trend some analysts—including myself—say is likely to continue along with the greener global Zeitgeist.

Perhaps the quintessential green product seller operating today is Gaiam (Nasdaq: GAIA). These guys bill themselves as "a lifestyle company," creating green-oriented media products and selling products such as green jewelry, organic cotton clothing and bed sheets, and eco-friendly patio furniture. A focus on personal development, wellness, spirituality, and, of course, living la vida verde are all part of Gaiam's niche. With Gaiam, you get the paradigmatic company selling to those who've made their commitment to the green way of life.

Toward the End of a Green Journey

I hope that up until this point in our green journey you've been exposed to a lot of new concepts, new companies, and new ways of thinking with respect to profiting from the Green Revolution. In the final chapter, we are going to look at ways that you can build a green portfolio. We'll also look at a few new ways of looking at what I think we'll be the inevitable push for greener and greener pastures.

CHAPTER

Building a Green Portfolio

A GREEN CALL TO ARMS

A wise man should have money in his head, but not in his heart.
—Jonathan Swift

In the preceding chapters we've covered quite a bit of technical territory. You've learned much about the overwhelming and truly massive wave of transformational change that is the Green Revolution.

We've covered the demographic, climate, security, and cost drivers that have helped sear a new green Zeitgeist into our global consciousness. We've also seen how government incentives and mandates—along with a whole lot of venture capital—has helped create a virtual green explosion just begging to be taken advantage of by an investing public hungry not only to be green, but to make green.

Finally, we've covered some of the best green sectors and learned about some of the top green companies providing solutions to the challenges in their respective areas. In my opinion, we can save the world and make a fortune. And what, I dare ask, is more important than that?

But before we can make a fortune by investing in green stocks, we have to lay down a few simple ground rules.

CAUTION: Green Portfolio Construction Ahead

Building profitable positions in the stocks mentioned in this book—or in any investments for that matter—takes disciplined buying.

This means you cannot go around chasing stocks exploding upward. Rather, you must buy them judiciously, and as they naturally settle below their price-trend support levels.

Disciplined buying also means "stepping into" your positions with one-third bites. Try not to roll the dice on a single barrage of buying in hopes of having the perfect timing. This isn't realistic, even for the best of the so-called "market timers."

In many cases, investing in alternative energy and other green stocks is risky. These stocks are often fast-moving, aggressive-growth stocks, and you should take that fact into consideration when deciding how much of your overall portfolio to allocate to any of the stocks in the various green sectors.

The companies we've discussed here do indeed have the potential for explosive growth that could make you life-changing wealth, but as the saying goes, with big reward comes big risk. Most of the stocks discussed in this book do come with a lot of volatility and a lot of risk. Of course, they also come complete with tremendous upside.

Because of the risk/reward situation in most of the stocks in the various green sectors, you have to choose your poison carefully. Show due diligence, look at the fundamental and the technical conditions in any stock you're considering, and enter into each position in small bites.

Those are just some of the basic rules I recommend in my ChangeWave Investing advisory service, and they've worked tremendously well for tens of thousands of investors over the past decade plus. This service tracks nearly all of the companies mentioned in this book, and we monitor market conditions to see which of these companies investors should own at any given moment.

If I've done my job here, by now you're likely champing at the bit to jump on and ride the green wave. Yet I must caution you not to dive in headfirst. Keep in mind that the stocks in these green sectors should comprise only a portion of your portfolio. They should by no means constitute a complete investment strategy.

All right, that's enough of my cautionary words on disciplined portfolio management. I mean, I doubt when you bought this book you did so to find out how to be careful with your investments. Now let's turn to one final aspect of this Green Revolution that I find irrepressibly compelling, and it has to do with one of my favorite topics—global capitalism.

The World Is Not Flat—It's Voracious

With all due respect to the brilliant *New York Times* columnist Thomas L. Friedman, the world is not flat as he claims in his 2005 bestselling and appropriately titled book, *The World Is Flat: A Brief History of the Twenty-First Century*. Not that I disagree with Friedman, but I think he underestimated the power of globalization. I'd say a better way to describe the globalization phenomenon is—the world is voracious. That is to say, the world harbors an absolutely ravenous desire to fulfill her global economic destiny.

I first realized this in, of all places, Las Vegas. As I was going from the airport to my hotel, I looked around and concluded that Sin City is really just one big bastion of capitalism. The myriad and grandiose hotels, casinos, shops, and restaurants are all a testament to the melding of ideas and capital. And even if you don't particularly like the Vegas experience, you've got to admit that it truly is an amazing example of capitalism incarnate.

But then I realized that this triumph of capitalism isn't only confined to a desert playground in America. All around the globe, capitalism is taking hold and driving the world in a newer, richer direction. In fact, the global capitalism boom is so huge it's actually displacing the United States as the coolest kid on the economic block.

Now before you get mad and blame the messenger, please hear me out. You see, as an investor and investment manager, I do not have the luxury of denial. Objectivity is the only true virtue when it comes to this business, and from my objective reading of the tea leaves I've come to the realization that the next great economic age of world history won't be centered on the United States.

This "Post-American Economic Age," as journalist Fareed Zakaria tells us in his book, *The Post-American World*, is all about the rise of the rest of the world. It is in no way an indication that America is headed to the scrap heap of history. As a matter of fact, it's the total reverse of that. This new economic age is not about the fall of capitalism. It's about its success and the way it is manifesting itself around the globe. You see, the United States has effectively exported capitalism, the most successful—and as the great novelist/philosopher Ayn Rand has said, the only *moral* social system—to the rest of the world. Equipped with this new economic paradigm, the rest of the world is now hell-bent on catching up to us. It is this amazing global race to make up for so much lost economic time that's changing the world for the better.

Before I go on, I want to give you a little history lesson. Here are the major stages of economic development to help put this Post-American Economic Age into context. The first modern economic age was the rise of Western civilization, when Western nations emerged as world powers. It began in the fifteenth century and cultivated much of the world we now know: science and technology, commerce and capitalism, agricultural and industrial revolutions.

The second great economic age, the age of Americanism, was the rise of the United States in the late nineteenth and early twentieth centuries. As the United States converted from an agrarian to an industrial economy, we grew our nation and its population to the greatest economic heights in history. We became a superpower of unheard-of size, influence, and strength.

In the next economic age, the post-American era, the rest of the global economy has imported much of the infrastructure and institutions of Western capitalism, and that has accelerated their growth.

We are now in the final chapter of the last economic age. The death of communism, the end of the Cold War, and the end of Maoism and China's rebirth have all sowed the seeds for the next great economic age.

The United States must now accept the economic reality that the rise of Western civilization and then of the United States was a dress rehearsal for the rise of the rest of the world. This new story is really one of size and scale. The countries that innovated and led the Western world were relatively small—the Dutch and their trading system, Britain and its industry. Modern economic miracles such as Denmark, Switzerland, and Ireland have populations smaller than most U.S. states.

The United States was the first major economic revolution to take place with a large population. The range and the depth of our prosperity have been unique up to this point. During the American economic age, China, Russia, India, and Brazil were basically asleep, either unwilling or unable to participate in the world economy. Now, they're awake and in a massive rush to catch up.

What makes this age different than the rise of the Western world or the United States is the scale: 3 billion people are awakening to capitalism at the very same time. This dwarfs the size and scale of the last two economic shifts.

And what does this new awakening mean to you, the investor looking to profit from the Green Revolution? In a word: opportunity.

You see, only those who understand (and acknowledge) the rise of the rest of the world will understand that this requires us to invest differently than we have in the past. Understand that the Post-American Age has Brazil, Russia, India, and China adding 20 million new middle-class households each year. This group will be five times larger than the Baby Boom generation, and they will start spending money right now.

As the world grows, so will its appetite for energy, food, and technology. That's really the key here. Think about what the world needs, then invest in the likely suspects ready to provide just that.

And what will the world need? Among other things, a big supply of affordable, renewable, and clean energy.

By using this book as your guide, you can understand the situation in many different green energy segments. With a little intellectual elbow grease—and maybe even a little help from ChangeWave Investing—you'll be well equipped to make sound investment decisions.

The One-Third Principle of ChangeWave Investing

In ChangeWave Investing, I advise you to enter into any stock position with about one-third of your desired investment. In upward-trending markets, you should place a good-until-canceled "buy stop" or buy order 5 percent to 10 percent *ahead* of your initial entry price to ensure you complete your position at a reasonable basis in the case of a runaway breakout to the positive, which is a common occurrence in bull markets for aggressive-growth stocks.

I also recommend you add an additional one-third of your capital to your initial positions if you get a 5 percent to 10 percent pullback from your initial entry price. Then wait and watch closely. If the position starts to move toward profitability, add your final one-third. If it starts sliding to 15 percent or more below your entry price, it may be time to sell it to contain your losses.

There is one caveat here: if, after investing your first portion, you get a more sizeable pullback (15 percent or more) where there is no *significant* change in your investment thesis, you should complete your remaining two-thirds position on that move.

I advise ChangeWave Investing subscribers to start taking positions at or under what we call the "buy under" price, that is to say, the top of what we think is an attractive price range for a specific stock.

(Continues)

(*Continued*)

Now, when I say "at or under," I want to make sure you understand that you don't ignore a stock if it hits the buy under price exactly.

The idea is to get into each stock gradually but to watch out for big moves downward. Institutional investors are getting into these stocks at the 20-day, 30-day, and 50-day moving averages. If a stock drops too far below its 50-day moving average, it's a sign that the company may have some major problem that you might not be aware of, and it may be time to pull out.

Now I realize that many of the ideas in this book are just that— only ideas. But ideas can be very powerful things. In fact, ideas are the only things that can truly move the world. Armed with an arsenal of ideas aimed at solving the world's energy and related challenges, humanity can mold her environment into a more livable, cleaner, greener, and even more financially rewarding state.

The way I see it, the choice is ours. If we are to prevail, our world must be shaped on the anvil of good ideas. Anything less is beneath the greatness we know mankind is capable of.

I hope that in some small way, this book has contributed to the fountainhead of human progress.

APPENDIX A

Master List of Green Companies

Throughout this book I've mentioned many individual companies, but the list of companies within each sector is by no means exhaustive. To help round out the list of public and selected private companies in each green sector, I've made a more comprehensive, if not complete, "master list." The stock exchange symbol for each is in parentheses. You can enter these symbols in the "get quotes" box of such online financial websites as Yahoo! Finance (finance.yahoo. com) and Google Finance (http://finance.google.com/finance).

Clean Transportation

A123 Systems (private)

Altair Nanotechnologies (ALTI)

Clean Diesel Technologies Inc. (CDTI)

Energy Conversion Devices (ENER)

Ford (F)

General Motors (GM)

Honda Motor Co. (HMC)

Hybrid Technologies, Inc. (HYBR.OB)

Tata Motors (TTM)

Tesla Motors (private)

Toyota Motor Corp. (TM)

Valence Technology (VLNC)

ZAP (ZAAP.OB)

Solar

Akeena Solar (AKNS)

Ascent Solar (ASTI)

China Sunergy Co. (CSUN)

DayStar Technologies (DSTI)

Energy Conversion Devices (ENER)

Evergreen Solar Inc. (ESLR)

First Solar (FSLR)

GT Solar International (SOLR)

JA Solar Holdings Co., Ltd. (JASO)

LDK Solar (LDK)

Real Goods Solar, Inc. (RSOL)

ReneSola (SOL)

SunPower (SPWR)

Suntech Power Holdings (STP)

Trina Solar (TSL)

Yingli Green Energy (YGE)

Water

American States Water (AWR)

American Water Works Company (AWK)

Aqua America (WTR)

Badger Meter Inc. (BMI)

Basin Water (BWTR)

Calgon Carbon (CCC)

Energy Recovery (ERII)

Flexible Solutions International Inc. (FSI)

Flowserve (FLS)

Gorman-Rupp (GRC)

Insituform Technologies Inc. (INSU)

Layne Christensen (LAYN)

Met-Pro (MPR)

Nalco (NLC)

PowerShares Water Resources (PHO)

Veolia Environnement (VE)

Waters Corp. (WAT)

Smart Grid

Beacon Power Corporation (BCON)

Comverge, Inc. (COMV)

Cooper Industries (CBE)

EnerNOC (ENOC)

ESCO Technologies (ESE)

Itron (ITRI)

Eco-Efficient IT

Citrix Systems (CTXS)

Microsoft (MSFT)

VMware (VMW)

Green Plastics

Archer Daniels Midland (ADM)

Cereplast (CERP.OB)

Metabolix (MBLX)

Biofuels

Aventine Renewable Energy (AVR)

Environmental Power Corp. (EPG)

Gushan Environmental Energy Limited (GU)

MGP Ingredients Inc. (MGPI)

Monsanto (MON)

New Generation Biofuels Holdings, Inc. (GNB)

Nova Biosource Fuels, Inc. (NBF)

O2Diesel Corp. (OTOD.OB)

Pacific Ethanol (PEIX)

Potash Corp. of Saskatchewan (POT)

The Andersons (ANDE)

VeraSun (VSE)

Xethanol Corp. (XNL)

Fuel Cells and Advanced Batteries

Ballard Power Systems (BLDP)

Bloom Energy (private)

Distributed Energy Systems (DESC)

Energy Conversion Devices (ENER)

Enova Systems Inc. (ENA)

FuelCell Energy (FCEL)

Lithium Technology Corp. (LTHU.PK)

Maxwell Technologies (MXWL)

Medis Technologies (MDTL)

Plug Power (PLUG)

Quantum Fuel Systems Technologies Worldwide (QTWW)

Ultralife Corp. (ULBI)

United Technologies (UTX)

Wind

A-Power Energy Generation Systems (APWR)

Broadwind Energy, Inc. (BWEN.OB)

Clipper Windpower (CWP.L)

Gamesa Corporacion Technologica (GAM.MC)

Suzlon Energy (SUZLON.NS)

Vestas Wind Systems (VWS.CO)

Zoltek (ZOLT)

Green Coal

Arch Coal (ACI)

Consol Energy (CNX)

Evergreen Energy (EEE)

Fuel Tech (FTEK)

Massey Energy (MEE)

Natural Resources Partners (NRP)

Peabody Energy (BTU)

Yanzhou Coal Mining Co. (YZC)

Green Buildings

American Superconductor Corporation (AMSC)

Capstone Turbine Corp. (CPST)

Cree, Inc. (CREE)

Echelon Corporation (ELON)

Johnson Controls (JCI)

Lighting Science Group Corporation (LSCG.OB)

Orion Energy Systems (OESX)

Natural Foods

Fresh Harvest Products, Inc. (FRHV.OB)

Gaiam (GAIA)

Green Mountain Coffee Roasters (GMCR)

Hain Celestial (HAIN)

Lifeway Foods Inc. (LWAY)

United Natural Foods (UNFI)

Whole Foods Market (WFMI)

B

Green Investing Resources

The information stream in the green investing arena is voluminous and ever evolving. Keeping up with all of the latest technology, company, and industry news is a daunting task. To help you get a handle on all the latest in the green field, I have put together this personal list of resources that I use to stay on top of all things green.

This list is by no means exhaustive. However, this selection will get you pointed in the right direction toward finding out what information you need when it comes to the greener end of the investing and technology spectrum.

ChangeWave Investing

www.changewave.com

Clean Edge

www.cleanedge.com

CNET News

www.cnet.com

Energy Information Administration

www.eia.doe.gov

Fox Business News

www.foxbusiness.com

Greentechmedia

www.greentechmedia.com

International Energy Agency

www.iea.org

Investor's Business Daily

www.investors.com

Renewable Fuels Association

www.ethanolrfa.org

SolarBuzz

www.solarbuzz.com

Sustainable Business.com

www.sustainablebusiness.com

Treehugger.com

www.treehugger.com

U.S. Green Building Council

www.usgbc.org

Wall Street Journal

www.wsj.com

Water Industry News

www.waterindustry.org

Yahoo! Finance

www.finance.yahoo.com

References

American Society of Civil Engineers. *Report Card for America's Infrastructure 2005.* Reston, VA: American Society of Civil Engineers, 2006.

BTM Consult. World Market Update 2007: International Wind Energy Development. Ringkøbing, Denmark: BTM Consult, 2008.

Department of Energy (DOE). "Solar Energy—An Advantage for the Building Industry." Washington, D.C.: National Renewable Energy Laboratory, January 2007.

Energy Information Administration (EIA). *International Energy Outlook 2007.* Report No.: DOE/EIA-0484(2007). Washington, D.C.: U.S. Department of Energy, May 2007.

Environmental Protection Agency (EPA). *EPA's 2008 Report on the Environment,* Chapter 3: "Water." Report No.: EPA/600/R-07/045F. Washington, D.C.: National Center for Environmental Assessment. Available at: http://www.epa.gov/roe.

Friedman, Thomas L. *The World Is Flat: A Brief History of the Twenty-First Century.* New York: Farrar, Straus and Giroux, 2005.

Greentech Media. *Venture Power Report.* Cambridge, MA, May 2008.

Makower, J.; Pernick, R.; and Wilder, C. *Clean-Energy Trends 2008.* San Francisco, CA: Clean Edge, March 2008.

National Energy Technology Laboratory (NETL). *A Vision for the Modern Grid.* Washington, D.C.: U.S. Department of Energy, March 2007.

Solar America Initiative (SAI). *A Plan for the Integrated Research, Development, and Market Transformation of Solar Energy Technologies.* Report No.: SETP-2006-0010. Washington, D.C.: U.S. Department of Energy, February 2007.

Solarbuzz. *Marketbuzz 2008: Annual World Solar Photovoltaic Industry Report.* San Francisco, CA: Solarbuzz, LLC, March 2008.

United Nations (UN). *Global Trends in Sustainable Energy Investment 2008 Report.* New York: UN, 2008.

U.S. Green Building Council (USGBC). *Green Building by the Numbers.* Washington, D.C.: USGBC, August 2008.

Wall Street Journal. "Review and Outlook: The Biofuels Backlash." May 7, 2008.

Wallerstein, N. *What Is the Evidence on Effectiveness of Empowerment to Improve Health?* Copenhagen, Denmark: Health Evidence Network, WHO Europe, February 2006. Available at: http://www.euro.who.int/Document/E88086.pdf.

Wiser, R.; Bolinger, M. *Annual Report on U.S. Wind Power Installation, Cost, and Performance Trends: 2007.* Report No. TP-500-41435; DOE/GO-102007-2433. Washington, D.C.: U.S. Department of Energy, May 2008. Available at: www.nrel.gov/docs/fy07osti/41435.pdf.

Zakaria, Fareed. *The Post-American World.* New York: W.W. Norton, 2008.

Index